ARIZONA LANDMARKS

Text by
James E. Cook

Edited by
Wesley Holden

Color Photography by
Arizona Highways Magazine Contributors

Design and Production by
W. Randall Irvine

(Front Page) Mission San Xavier del Bac, "the White Dove of the Desert," is the most famous of Father Eusebio Francisco Kino's missions. Today San Xavier, south of Tucson, is an active mission to the Papago Indians. In this artistic rendition, the setting sun and mission skyline are reflected in a partial double image. Willard Clay

(Pages 2 and 3) The San Francisco Peaks, tallest in Arizona, are most majestic when their snow cover is contrasted against a deep blue sky. Peter Bloomer

(Pages 4 and 5) A combination of sunlight and storm creates a rainbow over Grand Canyon, photographed from the South Rim. Kathleen Norris Cook

(Pages 6 and 7) The Navajo call this natural arch in Monument Valley the Ear of the Wind. A Navajo woman and daughter move their flock to better grass. Ray Manley Studios

Arizona Landmarks was prepared by the Related Products Development section of Arizona Highways magazine, a monthly publication of the Arizona Department of Transportation. Hugh Harelson, Publisher/Wesley Holden, Managing Editor/ Robert J. Farrell, Associate Editor Related Product Development.

Library of Congress Catalog Number 84-73392
ISBN 0 916179 04 4

Printed in Japan

Table of Contents

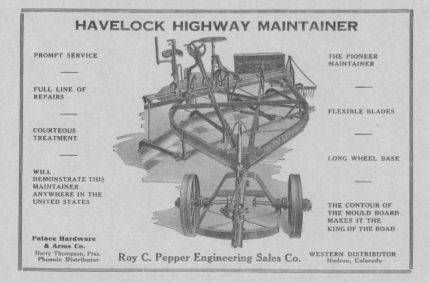

HAVELOCK HIGHWAY MAINTAINER

PROMPT SERVICE

FULL LINE OF
REPAIRS

COURTEOUS
TREATMENT

WILL
DEMONSTRATE THIS
MAINTAINER
ANYWHERE IN THE
UNITED STATES

THE PIONEER
MAINTAINER

FLEXIBLE BLADES

LONG WHEEL BASE

THE CONTOUR OF
THE MOULD BOARD
MAKES IT THE
KING OF THE ROAD

Palace Hardware
& Arms Co.
Harry Thompson, Pres.
Phoenix Distributor

Roy C. Pepper Engineering Sales Co.

WESTERN DISTRIBUTOR
Hudson, Colorado

(Top) Workers at the mill for the King of Arizona Mine in Yuma County, 1900. The mine gives its initials to the Kofa Mountains. Arizona State Library and Archives

(Left and below) Arizona Highways grew from this modest beginning in April, 1925, with vendors of road-building products supporting the magazine for the first dozen years. Topics included, among others, "The Engineer's Log," "Expansion Joints — Their Use in Arizona," and a travelog about a trip "From Yuma to Phoenix Over Good Roads."

Fortunately, landmarks belong to maps and not to calendars. Landmarks remain, while people move past in waves and cycles (and recently in Winnebagos). The San Francisco Peaks not only have the highest summit in Arizona but stand up sharply as mountains should, visible for maybe 100 miles against a clear blue sky. The Peaks are home to some of the Kachinas, the Hopi gods represented by colorful Kachina dolls. Those same peaks, and Navajo Mountain on the Arizona-Utah border, are points on the spiritual compass by which the Navajo relate to the Universe. And even before the Navajo and Hopi, people the anthropologists call Anasazi carved petroglyphs of their landmarks on the rocks.

In 1540, Francisco Vásquez de Coronado, searching for the golden cities of Cíbola, heard of a vast gorge northwest of the Zuñi and Hopi pueblos. Coronado sent Captain García López de Cárdenas and a party of soldiers to investigate what would become Arizona's best-known landmark, the Grand Canyon.

Pedro de Castañeda, a member of the Coronado expedition who kept a meticulous diary, told how Cárdenas sent a party of the most agile men down toward the Colorado River "which looked from above as though the water was six feet wide across, although the Indians said it was half a league wide."

Feldman   Tucson, Arizona.

Tumacacori Mission, north of Nogales, was a ruin for more than a century. Arizona State Library and Archives

The men struggled a third of the way into the Canyon, but returned defeated. They reported that "the river seemed very large from the place which they had reached, and that from what they saw they thought the Indians had given the width correctly. Those who stayed above had estimated that some huge rocks on the sides of the cliffs seemed to be about as tall as a man, but those who went down swore that when they reached those rocks they were bigger than the great tower of Seville."

The deceptive scale of Arizona landmarks is a recurring theme in state lore, and a rich source of humor. Historian and storyteller Marshall Trimble illustrates it with a yarn that goes something like this:

A guest at a dude ranch told the cowboys he was going to hike to a mountain on the horizon.

"But it's twenty miles to that mountain," one of the wranglers warned.

The dude replied that it couldn't be that far, and began walking. Several hours later, the crew got worried about the visitor and set out to locate him. They found him beside a rivulet, taking off his clothes.

"What are you doin' that for?"

"I'm going to swim this river."

"Why that stream's not more than six inches wide."

Said the dude, "I was fooled once, but I'll not be fooled again."

Since Cárdenas, millions of people have expressed their disbelief at the scale of the Grand Canyon. They do so conveniently, if not routinely, for getting to know the canyon even briefly is not a routine experience.

It takes a native several years to realize that Arizona's physical wonders are also spiritual landmarks for people around the world. During all of this century, knowing people "burned out" by urban society have found serenity in a desert which at first appears forbidding.

During the 1920s, Dick Wick Hall's humorous accounts of life in the little town of Salome, Arizona, were avidly read by subscribers to the *Saturday Evening Post* and newspapers across the nation. While other famous Americans recuperated at the Arizona Biltmore in Phoenix or one of the state's dude ranches, Hall operated a Laughing Gas Station for motorists. Hall poked fun at the world through the mimeographed pages of the *Salome Sun*, and told of his pet frog who was seven years old and had never learned to swim.

Salome was not, and is not, famed as a place of scenic grandeur, but in a rare bit of serious writing, Hall explained: "The wonderful peace and quiet of it, which only the dweller of the desert can understand and appreciate. (Omitting verbs was one of Hall's endearing qualities.) Here, at last, I thought, is one place where I can do as I please and no one to bother me, where I can get acquainted with myself and find the something that every man in his own soul is consciously or unconsciously searching for—himself."

Landmarks and mileposts. In 1925, the Arizona Highway Department began publishing a monthly bulletin called *Arizona Highways.* Its beginning was little more auspicious than the carving of V13 on a rock. It carried reports on the conditions of Arizona's primitive highway system and called for bids on construction.

Businesses which expected to sell goods and services to the highway department advertised liberally. The Portland cement suppliers and their competitors, vendors of asphaltic cement, bought full pages. So did the makers of newfangled corrugated steel culverts.

Editors filled odd holes in the magazine with file photographs of Arizona's landmarks: Tumacacori Mission, Wonderland of Rocks in the Chiricahua Mountains, Oak Creek Canyon. Soon, hometown boosters were writing articles promoting local attractions around the state. Some of these wonders never became anything more than points of local pride: in the White Mountains, a forest of dwarf trees apparently grew tall before they grew famous; and near Safford, an eroded amphitheater called Red Knolls gained only local acclaim. But through the pages of *Arizona Highways,* other Arizona landmarks became known around the world.

During its first dozen years, each issue of *Arizona Highways* carried a full-page map showing the status of the road system. Gradually, season by season, black bars representing pavement snaked across the map.

Evolution of the magazine also was gradual, but it had its own milestones. The first color cover appeared in July, 1937, shortly before the road condition maps ceased. In 1938, Raymond Carlson became editor, bringing a grace and intellect that made *Arizona Highways* a landmark in American publishing. Advertising disappeared and editorial color expanded. The magazine has boasted, and no one has contested it, that in December, 1946, *Arizona Highways* produced the first magazine in history with full color on every page. Holiday issues came to be so special that subscribers around the world still await their arrival.

The success of the magazine undoubtedly had much to do with the phenomenal growth of Arizona, especially since World War II. People who had experienced Arizona only through the magazine, or the movies, or perhaps a Zane Grey novel, were assigned to one of dozens of military training bases built quickly at the beginning of World War II. Many returned after the war. Today, there are nine times as many people in the state as there were in 1925. The highway system has matured beyond the fondest forecasts of those early road boosters. In 1932, a highway engineer returned from a national conference and wrote an article for *Arizona Highways* about the highways of the future. Although he wrote about limited access, multilane highways, he could not have anticipated the interstate highways that cross Arizona.

Generations pass the landmarks like a mark on a wagon wheel. Those who once celebrated each new mile of pavement watched in amazement as new cycles of Arizonans (in some cases Arizonans with new cycles) sought out the dirt roads to seek challenge and solitude. Even today there is no shortage of either. Arizona still has an incomprehensible supply of space.

Thirteen-mile Rock sits beside pavement now and is duly noticed by historians. The wagon road it marked is, for a few miles, a highway. A knowing traveler can take the road from Interstate 17 past Thirteen-mile Rock to the quiet of the Mogollon Rim and the Colorado Plateau, looking for tranquility, or spectacle, or maybe for himself.

James E. Cook

(Right) Arizona Highways magazine's first color cover was in 1937.

(Far right) The December, 1946, issue, the first all-color issue of any magazine, featured a cover photograph by Barry Goldwater.

(Below right) The tower at Desert View, Grand Canyon, as it looks today. Bob Clemenz

(Below) The picture and masthead from page 1 of the March, 1954, Arizona Highways magazine are reproduced in their entirety. Editor Raymond Carlson's name first appeared in 1938, and he shaped the magazine for more than 30 years. George Avey was the art editor for twenty-five of those years. Other than the addition of Joseph Stacey as associate editor in 1967, this compact editorial staff remained the same until Carlson's retirement in 1971.

(Following panel, pages 14-15) The Mogollon Rim, south edge of the Colorado Plateau, helps define Arizona's regions. This view, from beside the Old Rim Road, or General Crook's Trail, hasn't changed much since Army wife Martha Summerhayes saw it from a wagon in 1874. James Tallon

VOL. XXX No. 3   MARCH 1954
RAYMOND CARLSON, Editor
GEORGE M. AVEY, Art Editor
HOWARD PYLE
Governor of Arizona

ARIZONA HIGHWAY COMMISSION

C. A. Calhoun, Chairman . . . . . Mesa
John M. Scott, Vice-Chairman . . Show Low
Fred D. Schemmer, Member . . . . Prescott
Frank E. Moore, Member . . . . Douglas
Grover J. Duff, Member . . . . . Tucson
Patrick C. Downey, Secretary . . . Phoenix
R. C. Perkins, State Hwy. Engr. . . Phoenix
Thad G. Baker, Special Counsel . . Phoenix

ARIZONA HIGHWAYS is published monthly by the Arizona Highway Department a few miles north of the confluence of the Gila and Salt in Arizona. Address: ARIZONA HIGHWAYS, Phoenix, Arizona. $3.00 per year in U. S. and possessions; $3.50 elsewhere; 35 cents each. Entered as second-class matter Nov. 5, 1941 at Post Office in Phoenix, under Act of March 3, 1879. Copyrighted, 1954, by Arizona Highway Department.

 115

Allow five weeks for change of addresses. Be sure to send in the old as well as new address.

ARIZONA HIGHWAYS Presents THE GRAND CANYON of Arizona

Love of the desert is an acquired taste. Since 1540, when Coronado began a stream of Spanish soldiers and missionaries crossing the Sonoran Desert, explorers have wondered at its apparent hostility and cataloged its intriguing complexities. There seems at first exposure to be too much expanse, too many sharp edges, too few green things and creature comforts. It takes a while to learn that Nature has compensated richly with intangibles man was not aware he could use.

The hostility is not an illusion. The desert can threaten the life of the careless newcomer. He may not learn to love it until he has seen the paloverde tree bloom golden above the subtler greens and browns of greasewood and mesquite, or watched a mama Gambel quail lead a row of chicks through the brush on a clear desert morning.

Up close, the desert can be charming. At a distance, it is mysterious, its purple mountains promising ancient secrets preserved by the crystal air.

Naturalist Joseph Wood Krutch spent most of his life in the Northeast. He had a world reputation as author, teacher, and social critic by the time he came to Tucson in the 1950s. Krutch found himself happier and healthier than ever before and spent the last quarter-century of his life on the desert. He explored, defined, and praised the desert in a critically literate fashion.

In *The Voice of the Desert*, published in 1954, he wrote: "So far as living things go, all this adds up to what even an ecologist may so far forget himself as to call an 'unfavorable environment.' But like all such pronouncements this doesn't mean much unless we ask 'unfavorable for what and for whom?' For many plants, for many animals, and for some men it is very favorable indeed. Many of the first two would languish and die, transferred to some region where conditions were 'more favorable.' It is here, and here only, that they flourish. Many men feel healthier and happier in the bright dry air than they do anywhere else...."

(Above) Driving the Camino del Diablo, Highway of the Devil, caravan-style in 1933 was chancy and required an overnight camp in the desert. Today over 100 miles of the old road are part of the sprawling Cabeza Prieta National Wildlife Refuge and Luke Air Force Bombing Range and closed to general travel. Tad Nichols

(Right above) If cars traveling the Old Plank Road met between turnouts, such as this one, one driver had to back up. Arizona Historical Society

(Right) Planks through the sand dunes kept travelers on the straight and narrow, and after wind storms sections of the road had to be dragged back to the surface. Arizona State Library and Archives

"The 'harsh' conditions they sometimes have to cope with appear to strangers much more difficult than they are, merely because they are not those to which a stranger is accustomed. After all, few environments are entirely favorable. No one out in a blizzard or ice storm in southern New England is likely to think of it as calculated to coddle man, beast, or vegetable...."

When an Arizonan complains about the 110-degree heat of an August afternoon, his neighbor from Connecticut is likely to answer with this bromide: "Yeah, but you don't have to shovel it."

Dick Wick Hall again, without Hall's tiresome capitals: "Out here in the desert you don't need much—and you don't get much either—and after a while you get so as you don't want much—and when you get that way there ain't much use in going somewhere else.... A man can put in a good deal of time setting and looking out across the desert, past miles and miles of greasewood and through the wriggly heat waves of the sunburned mountains in the distance, setting there just the same as you are, waiting for something to happen.

"After awhile you get so as you are just about the same as the mountains, only they have set there a little longer than most of us.... Whoever it was that said a thousand years is like a day and a day like a thousand years, he knew his cactus and said about all there is to say about the desert."

Even in this age of ready information, when *Arizona Highways* has been telling the world otherwise for sixty years, a few visitors come expecting the Arizona desert to match their expectations of the Gobi, or the simple lines of a Roadrunner cartoon. The cartoons are accurate only in the vividness of the colors and the peculiar behavior of the roadrunner. There is certainly desolation, and even a few sand dunes. Spanish explorers in the 1700s used a bleak route along the southern edge of the state. This route earned the label *El Camino del Diablo*, the Highway of the Devil, or *Camino del Muerto*, Highway of Death. It is recorded that hundreds did die along the route, including gold seekers flocking to California from 1849 to 1860.

Just beyond the California border, west of Yuma, stretch sand dunes and preserved remnants of a plank road, built in sections and laid out on the sand to allow early automobiles to cross. The road was one car wide. Ruby Cook of Yarnell, Arizona, remembers traveling the plank road for the first time in 1919. Her father drove a 1917 Model T touring car. "Sometimes it was better to travel that road at night," she recalls. "Then you could see the lights of the other cars coming and know when you needed to use one of the turnouts. It was a long way between two turnouts, and if two cars met on the planks, one had to back up."

That is not the kind of desert most people fall in love with, or the kind Krutch scrutinized with fascination and fond whimsy. Krutch sensed that to comprehend the vastness, one had to study the most minute components of rock, plant, and animal. He marveled at the road-runner, a member of the cuckoo family that acts somewhat in keeping with his cartoon caricature. And Krutch decried the fact the giant saguaro cactus has become a symbol of desert just anywhere, when, in fact, it grows only on the Sonoran Desert of Arizona and northern Mexico (plus a few in California, just across the Colorado River from Arizona).

In 1860, a New York-born geologist named Raphael Pumpelly was sent from Cincinnati to manage the Santa Rita mines south of Tucson. Pumpelly wrote:

"It was here that I first saw the effect of an extremely dry and transparent atmosphere. All the ravines and rocks of the Santa Rita Mountains are distinctly visible from Tucson, a distance of more than thirty miles; and in the very dry season, as at the time of my first visit, the tall pines on the summit could be clearly distinguished standing out against the sky.

"Accustomed to judgment of heights and distances in the atmosphere of the eastern states and Europe, I did not hesitate, on being first asked to guess the distance, to place it at less than ten miles."

lore about the Gila monster. Even in the hysteria of a first encounter, the scorpion has not grown much beyond the size of a man's hand.

What the visitor is more likely to see are ground squirrels, desert tortoises, gophers, coyotes, and mule deer. With great luck, he may see a collared peccary, or

when the season starts, though."

Coveralls: "Plenty of mule deer up there, too. Wonder where they find water?"

Rancher: "There's water there if you know where to look."

Coveralls: "I guess *they* know."

(Left) The towering saguaro's surprisingly shallow root system lets the cactus rapidly absorb water from occasional desert storms, then store it in its accordion-like body and arms. John L. Blackford

(Right) The organ pipe cactus is a rare species. In the U. S. it is confined to the area of Organ Pipe Cactus National Monument along the Mexican border. Ansel Adams

*"No. 2—the shortest hole on the courst—is not quite fifteen miles....
but I figger the lack of distance is more than offset
by the fact this hole is uphill all the way."*

Dick Wick Hall died in 1926, shortly after *Arizona Highways* was founded. He would have liked the magazine; in addition to being a humorist with the soul of a poet, he was a booster. The *Salome Sun* constantly sniped at county supervisors in faraway Yuma over the need for better roads in the northern part of Yuma County. U. S. Route 60-70 through Salome did become the main route from Phoenix to Los Angeles—until it was bypassed in the 1970s by Interstate 10. In 1983, Hall's part of Yuma County became La Paz County, the first secession in Arizona since Greenlee County was carved from Graham County in 1909.

In its early years, *Arizona Highways* periodically presented bits of Hall's writing. His fanciful Greasewood Golf Lynx preceded by several years the more famous Bar X Golf Course created by writer and artist Ross Santee.

Hall's fictitious course was "a little over twenty-three miles around," he wrote, and there was no need to manufacture hazards, since nature provided plenty. Hall's advertisements in the *Salome Sun* warned: "All caddys and horses lost on the course must be paid for."

Santee, a working cowboy and an *Arizona Highways* contributor, dreamed up a more ambitious course when he published *The Bar X Golf Course* in 1933. Dad Jackson was the fictitious owner of a ranch, looking for new ways to bring in revenue. Dad explained the course hole-by-hole:

"No. 2—the shortest hole on the courst—is not · quite fifteen miles. I know this hole is short but I figger the lack of distance is more than offset by the fact this hole is uphill all the way an' a dude must pack his own water. No dude will be allowed to start the hole without a full canteen.... Where Black Canyon cuts in about ten miles up is what really makes it sporty. By carrying the canyon on his shot a dude can cut off at least two miles."

The latest appearance of the Bar X in *Arizona Highways* was in January, 1983, an issue devoted to the state's real-life golf courses. Santee's sketches, and Dad Jackson's calculations, were fifty years old and still fresh.

Each lover of the desert celebrates in his own way. Krutch, after 200 pages of appraisal, summed up more eloquently this last frontier: "It is the last because it was the latest reached, but it is the last also because it is, in many ways, a frontier which *cannot* be crossed. It brings man up against his limitations, turns him in upon himself, and suggests values which more indulgent regions minimize. Sometimes it inclines to contemplation men who have never contemplated before."

(Right) A photographer's look at Ross Santee's hole number two. This view of saguaro and cholla cactus, with Roosevelt Lake in the distance, is near Tonto National Monument. Ed Cooper

(Following panel, pages 26-27) John Mix Stanley was a draftsman, in 1846, with a detachment of the Corps of Topographic Engineers under Lt. William Emory—part of General Stephen Kearny's Army of the West. He was the first established American artist to travel to Arizona, and his duty was to accurately depict the landscape through which they passed and later make lithographic reproductions for the expedition report. Nine years later, when he painted Chain of Spires Along the Gila River, he substituted the deer in an Edenesque setting for an encampment of soldiers that he pictured in the lithograph. The exact location of the Stanley painting is several miles northwest of Florence, Arizona. Stanley's works were on display in a wing of the Smithsonian Institution in 1865 when that wing burned. All but five were destroyed, another reason this painting of that particular landmark time and place is so highly prized. Courtesy Phoenix Art Museum; Museum Purchase

(Above) Theodore Roosevelt Dam under construction in 1909.
Salt River Project

(Right) The dam as it is today. Larry Ulrich

(Below) Former President Theodore Roosevelt, responsible for the reclamation project, arrived for its dedication in 1911.
Salt River Project

(Bottom) Spillway gates had not yet been installed when this 1919 photograph was taken. Arizona State Library and Archives

Lake Havasu, behind Parker Dam on the Colorado River,
is an important recreation spot for Californians as well as Arizonans.

(Inset) In 1968, developer Robert McCulloch Sr. purchased London
Bridge and shipped it stone block by stone block to the newly developing
community of Lake Havasu City. It has become one of Arizona's most
popular man-made landmarks. Carlos Elmer photos

(Above) The Mohave, the only twin-stack steamboat to operate on the Colorado River, was decked out for a May Day celebration at Yuma in 1876. Arizona Historical Society

(Left) On April 28, 1876, Mayor A.J. Finley troweled the cornerstone into place, and the Yuma Territorial Prison, which was to become known as the "Hellhole of Arizona," became a reality. Built with prison labor, it housed the worst criminals of the most lawless period in American history for thirty-three years. Of the 3069 people who were imprisoned here, twenty-nine were women, including the "heartless" Pearl Hart. Gatling guns were mounted in the towers, and there were few prison breaks, mostly from work details outside the walls, and even fewer successes. Today, Yuma Territorial Prison State Park is a landmark to the fierce law of those frontier days. Jeff Gnass

(Right) A 1949 photograph of the remains of the Old Plank Road through the sand dunes near Yuma. William Winter Irvine

Sunset at Saguaro National Monument. (Inset) The golden poppy, beautiful in isolation, sometimes carpets the Sonoran Desert after a wet winter.
Willard Clay photos

Fourteen miles west of Tucson lies one of the most innovative zoos in the world. It's called the Arizona-Sonora Desert Museum. In 1982, The New York Times featured it among the ten best zoos in the world, describing it as "…the most distinctive zoo in the United States." But the Desert Museum is more than a zoo. It is as much a botanical garden and geological interpretive center as it is a zoological landmark.

(Above) The Earth Sciences Center houses the mineral and geology exhibits. The mineral specimens from the Sonoran Desert are the finest in the world. Harry Redl

(Right) The playful river otters are popular with visitors. The exhibit includes a glassed-in underwater viewing area. James Tallon

(Far right) Another visitor favorite is the Lizard Exhibit at the main entrance to Arizona-Sonora Desert Museum. On sunny days, the warmth-loving reptiles pose for photographers by the hour. Harry Redl

(Below right) More than 300 species of Sonoran Desert plants are found on the grounds of the museum. Gill Kenny

(Below) Other small animals that visitors often enjoy for an entire afternoon are the prairie dogs. Tails wagging, they playfully pop in and out of the ground, but sentinels are ever alert. James Tallon

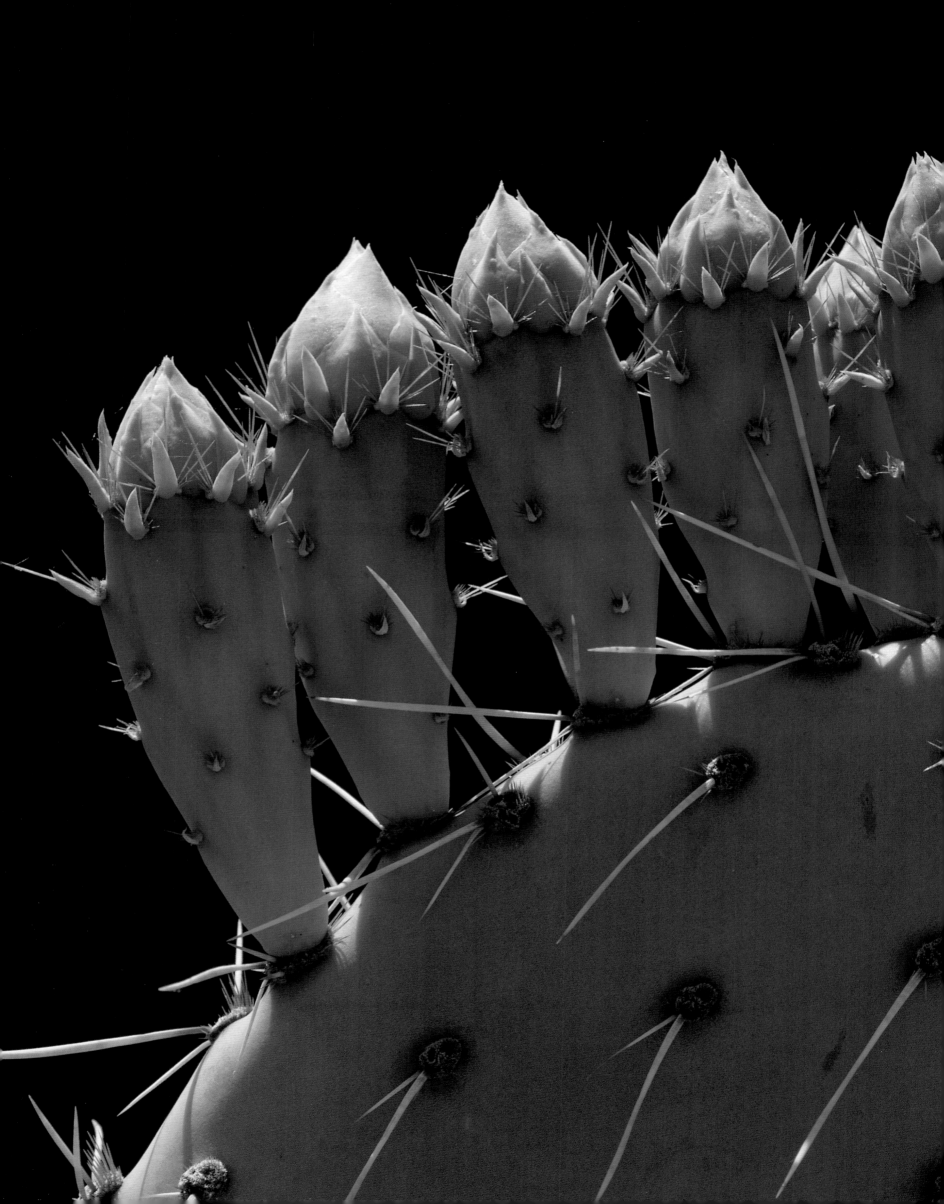

Father Eusebio Francisco Kino arrived in Pimeria Alta (what is now northern Sonora, Mexico, and southern Arizona) in 1687. Maps of that time showed this area as "tierra incognita," the unknown land. Father Kino established twenty-four missions before his death in 1711. But more than that, he was a scholar, scientist, geographer, builder, cattleman, administrator, and farmer who taught the Indians new ways to grow crops.

(Above) "Padre Kino Brings Cattle to the Altar Valley," by Ted De Grazia. Courtesy De Grazia Foundation

(Right) Tumacacori Mission, as it was photographed by Ansel Adams for an article in the November, 1952, Arizona Highways. Nancy Newhall's text tells an interesting story of how, in 1853, the United States bought this mountainous desert strip from Mexico...new settlers brought with them a fever for gold...legends of hidden treasure began to weave around the ruins of Tumacacori...and how Apache raids, it was believed, caused the priests to hide their ecclesiastic jewels and flee for their lives.

(Left) The annual Tumacacori Festival is held the first Sunday of December. The ceremonies commemorate Father Kino's first mass in this area. James Tallon

(Previous panel, pages 38-39) In spring the prickly pear cactus, bristling with spines and topped with beautiful flowers, both fascinates and repels. Willard Clay

THE SHELL OF TUMACACORI

Above: FACADE AND BELLTOWER
—AFTERNOON

PHOTOGRAPHED by ANSEL ADAMS
DESCRIBED by NANCY NEWHALL

The mission at Tumacacori today is a ruin and a shrine. The people who built these massive walls, who kneeled on the floor they had made to hear their own choir sing above, for whom the bells in the arches of this never-finished tower rang morning and evening, were driven from their ancestral hills and river lands more than a century ago, and their pueblo has sunk back into the earth.

A shell, formed and abandoned by the forces of history, eroded by the forces of the earth, Tumacacori still rises in the sunlight a monument to a hope.

Left: NICHE AND PILASTERS
—NOON

THE PUEBLO OF TUMACACORI enters history with a prayer.

In January, 1691, word flew up the valley of the Santa Cruz River that at Tucubavia there were two of the white men in black robes who came riding on great glossy beasts as fleet as deer to bring a wealth of new flocks and herds, wheat and strange blossoming fruit trees, to those who would kneel before a cross. This cross was not, as for the Indians, the symbol of the morning and the evening stars, nor was it clad with the downy feathers of the breath of life. On the white men's cross there hung a dying man, and with him a new heaven and a new hell, a new blessing and a new magic, with singing and lifelike images, brilliant in gold and satin.

PAGE FIVE • ARIZONA HIGHWAYS • NOVEMBER, 1952

For over 600 years, Casa Grande (Big House) has withstood the challenges of desert winds and infrequent but violent rains. Visitors to this prehistoric landmark cannot help but see a tribute to the industry and skills of a past people. It is possible that these people, the Hohokam, migrated to this area as early as 300 B.C. from far down in Mexico. They built hundreds of miles of canals to water their fields of maize, beans, squash, and cotton, and their cultural remains include fine quality pottery and carved shell jewelry. Anthropologists can only guess what happened to the Hohokam between 1400 and the early 1700s, but most authorities agree that today's Pima probably are their descendants.

(Above) Casa Grande as it must have appeared to early Spanish explorers of the Southwest.
Arizona State Library and Archives

(Right) Hohokam artifacts are from the collection at Casa Grande Ruins National Monument.
Jerry Jacka

(Far right) The mysterious four-story Casa Grande ruin was once part of a Hohokam community built about A.D. 1300-1350. Recent studies, as reported in the October, 1981, Arizona Highways, indicated the structure may have been used for astronomic observations. The National Park Service has protected this unique prehistoric landmark since 1918. James Tallon

(Above) The high-rise buildings of downtown Phoenix stand against a desert sunset. James Tallon

(Right) Arizona's original copper-domed capitol was begun in 1898 and dedicated in 1901. Its modern annex is in the background. Jerry Jacka

(Below) An aerial view of the state capitol was featured in the January, 1929, issue of National Geographic. McLaughlin Historical Collection

(Above) Camelback Mountain is the premier landmark of the Phoenix metropolitan area. During this century, the city has moved outward to envelop the mountain. William Sperry's recent photo of Camelback from the Arizona Country Club duplicated the location (right), about 1910, when this photograph caught a farmer working in his field. McLaughlin Historical Collection

(Opposite page) Although civilization is crowding in, Echo Canyon in Camelback Mountain retains much of the allure in the photograph by William Sperry (top) that it promised when R. C. Proctor photographed it more than forty years ago.

ARIZONA
HIGHWAYS
MARCH · 1948

(Far left) A hedgehog cactus blooms in the Superstition wilderness area.
Jerry Sieve

(Above) A Gambel's quail cock poised near a strawberry hedgehog cactus.
James Tallon

(Left) "Ho! Hum! It's Spring!" noted the editorial, and R. C. and Claire
Meyer Proctor provided the story and photos for a portfolio about the
desert in bloom. Readers response was enthusiastic, and throughout the
years, articles about the colors of an Arizona spring have become
a tradition.

(Following panel, pages 50-51) A crown of blossoms graces a barrel
cactus. Evening glow on the Sonoran Desert in southern Arizona.
Willard Clay photos

Cochise Head
as seen from Bonita Canyon
Chiricahua. Mts. Ariz.
Photo by Irwin

(Above) Cochise Head, the profile in repose at upper right, is a landmark of the Chiricahua Mountains. Photos such as this appeared frequently in early issues of Arizona Highways. Better known, however, are the whimsical rock shapes of Bonita Canyon, foreground, carved by wind and water from volcanic rocks. Arizona State Library and Archives

(Above right) Construction of the bridge over Salt River Canyon in the 1930s was a major event in the history of Arizona's road system. The winding ten-mile piece of U. S. Route 60 built through the canyon at that time cut several hours off the trip from Phoenix to the White Mountains and northeastern Arizona. Arizona State Library and Archives

Naturalist Joseph Wood Krutch wrote, "Scores of separate ranges, each with a name of its own, are sprinkled here and there, and in the southern part of the state they often rise abruptly from the desert floor itself. In fact it is nearly impossible to move anywhere so far away from them that the horizon is not ringed around with peaks .... Many are higher than any summit east of the Mississippi."

Losing sight of any kind of mountain can unsettle an Arizonan who goes to the flatlands. I drove diagonally across Mississippi one day. Because I could see nothing higher than the treetops, I suffered all day from the illusion that I must be on top of a mountain and would soon begin the drive down the other side. The following day, we drove through a limestone cut in eastern Tennessee and my wife said, "That's what I've been missing—rocks!"

To understand the White Mountains—in fact, to understand Arizona—it is helpful to know about a geological landmark called the Mogollon Rim (pronounced "muggy-OWN"). In one form or another, the Mogollon escarpment runs diagonally across Arizona, starting at its waistline on the New Mexico border and extending to the area of Hoover Dam on the opposite border. The Rim was named for Juan Ignacio Flores Mogollon, military governor of this part of New Spain from 1712 to 1715.

The Rim has many faces. At its most imposing, it is a cliff 2000 feet high, separating the Colorado Plateau on the north from the Tonto Basin region made famous by novelist Zane Grey. Geologists call this the Tonto section of the Rim. When Arizonans talk of the Rim and the "Rim Country," they usually are speaking of this rugged terrain immediately west of the White Mountains.

In effect, the east end of the Rim is the southern boundary of the White Mountains. Spanish explorers referred to these mountains as "Sierra Blanca," apparently because of a snow cap on the higher peaks. Early Americans called the region the Black Forest, possibly because of the dark green of the ponderosa pine which covers much of the range.

White Mountain Apaches have occupied the mountains for centuries. They fought fiercely in the nineteenth century to continue living there. The Fort Apache Indian Reservation occupies much of the mountains. The Apache-Sitgreaves National Forest takes in most of the rest.

The White Mountains rise from a 6000- or 7000-foot base on the Colorado Plateau to an elevation of 11,590 feet atop Mount Baldy, second highest point in Arizona. Hundreds of miles of creek drain the mountains in two directions, carving steep canyons as they go. On the south side of the range, Black River and White River combine to form the Salt River. On the north slope, streams flow into the Little Colorado River, which meanders across the plateau to join the Colorado River at the east end of the Grand Canyon.

Trout in the White Mountain streams have not escaped notice by generations of fishermen. Beginning in 1956, the White Mountain Apaches built dozens of small lakes on these mountain streams to attract tourists to the reservation. Today their efforts to serve tourists are concentrated on Sunrise, a growing ski complex just off State Route 260 between Springerville and Show Low.

The first ten years of *Arizona Highways* coincided with an important era of road building. The highway boosters of the White Mountains lobbied for their share.

The Coronado Trail (now part of U. S. Route 666), from Clifton to Springerville, was dedicated with a huge party at Hannagan Meadow on top of the Rim in 1927. *Arizona Highways* reported, "There will be a free barbeque of beef and bear with plenty of everything else to make up a sumptuous meal sufficient to feed the thousands expected from everywhere."

The road, paralleling the New Mexico border, is a spectacularly scenic route over some of the roughest Arizona mountains, but not a logical route for most Arizona traffic.

Today, U.S. Route 60, which goes from the White Mountains to Globe by way of Salt River Canyon, is a more popular route. That route was only a dream in 1917, when my paternal grandfather drove a Willys 70 into the state with a wife, four sons, and a dog. It took them ten days to get from Denver to Phoenix, the last four or five just to travel from Springerville to Phoenix. They crossed White River and Black River on wooden bridges a few miles east of where the White and the Black join to become Salt River. The road continued south to Rice, where San Carlos is now located, then to Globe, Roosevelt, and into Phoenix over the Apache Trail.

Periodically in the mid-30s, *Arizona Highways* reported on construction of the new route through spectacular Salt River Canyon and the curved steel bridge at the bottom. Crossing the gorge is a scenic treat for the motorist who is not an acrophobe. At a leisurely pace, it's four or five hours from Springerville to Phoenix.

That highway, as much as anything, separates the White Mountains from the Mogollon Rim Country to the west.

The Code of the West

I

Of the many problems that had beset Mary
Stockwell during her two years of school teaching
in the sparsely settled Tonto Basin
of Arizona, this last one was the knottiest,
the one that touched her most keenly. For it
involved her little sister, Georgiana May, who
to Arizona to be cured, the
a slight tendency

is on her way — will arrive in
9th Let me see. Goodness, that's tomorrow

ZANE GREY
UNDER THE TONTO RIM

83534-3 POCKET

1

OF THE MANY problems that had beset Mary
Stockwell during her two years of teaching school in the sparsely settled Tonto Basin of Arizona, this last one was the knottiest, the one that touched her most keenly. For it involved her little sister, Georgiana May, who was on her way to Arizona to be cured, the letter from their mother disclosed, of a slight tendency toward tuberculosis, and a very great leaning toward indiscriminate flirtation.

This day Mary was unusually tired. She had walked all the way up to the little log school-house on Tonto Creek—six miles and back again to the Thurman ranch at Green Valley, where she boarded. Her eighteen pupils, ranging from six-year-old Mytie Thurman to sixteen-year-old Richard, had broken all records that day for insubordination. Then the hot sun of the September afternoon and the thick dust of the long dry road through brush and forest had taxed her to extreme weariness. Consequently she was not at her best to receive such a shock as her mother's letter had given her.

"Well, there's no help for it," she thought wearily, taking up her letter again. "Georgiana is on her way—will arrive in Globe on the ninth. Let me see. Goodness, that's tomorrow—Tuesday. The mail stage leaves Globe on Wednesday. She'll get to Ryson about five o'clock. And I can't get away. I'll have to send someone to meet her. . . . Dear little golden-haired Georgie!"

Mary Stockwell seemed divided between distress at this sudden serious responsibility, and a reviving tender memory of her sister. What would she do with her? How would the Thurmans take this visit? Georgiana had looked very much like an angel, but she most assuredly had belied her appearance. Taking up the letter again, the perplexed schoolmistress hurried to

1

Zane Grey set many of his Western novels in the Rim area and wrote some of them in a cabin below the Rim near Tonto Creek. Grey was not the first nor the last to refer to the area below the Rim as the Tonto Basin, although it is not a basin in the usual sense of the word. The confused reader who wants to explore this further may find help in a book published in 1983, *Arizona's Names (X Marks the Place)*, by Dr. Byrd Howell Granger. The book, published as *Arizona Place Names* in 1935 and first updated in 1960, represents the combined work of the late historian Will C. Barnes and Dr. Granger, a retired University of Arizona professor.

The areas both above and below the Rim are cut with steep canyons, one set draining into the tributary system of the Salt River, the other into the Little Colorado River. General Crook's military road picked its way along the narrow Rim between the two watersheds to avoid the worst of the canyons.

In 1874, Martha Summerhayes was one of a few daring women who chose to accompany their Army husbands to the frontier. In her book *Vanished Arizona*, not published until 1908, she wrote of riding in an ambulance in the first wagon train to travel Crook's Road from Fort Verde to Fort Apache.

"The scenery was wild and grand; in fact, beyond all that I had ever dreamed of; more than that, it seemed so untrod, so fresh, somehow, and I do not suppose that even now, in the days of railroads and tourists, many people have had the view of the Tonto Basin which we had one day from the top of the Mogollon Range.

"I remember thinking, as we alighted from our ambulances and stood looking over into the Basin, 'Surely I have never seen anything to compare with this—but oh! would any sane human being voluntarily go through with what I have endured on this journey, in order to look upon this wonderful scene?' "

Mrs. Summerhayes could not have envisioned the numbers of people who would come to Arizona and travel nearly every inch of it. Yet the terrain has slowed

(Above left) *Zane Grey's cabin, about twenty-five miles east of Payson, has been restored and is open to the public. Herb and Dorothy McLaughlin*

(Above) *Zane Grey is pictured here on a hunting expedition in the area beneath the Mogollon Rim, called the Tonto Rim in Grey's famous novel.*

(Far left) *Zane Grey's handwritten draft of the beginning of* Code of the West *and the front cover of* Under the Tonto Rim, *two of Grey's many books about the Tonto Basin area below the Mogollon Rim, where he lived and wrote. McLaughlin Historical Collection*

visits to the Rim. Crook's Trail is still there in places, but civilization chose to parallel it below the Rim with State Route 260 rather than make a boulevard across the heads of all those canyons.

The ponderosa forest which covers much of the White Mountains and the Rim Country extends across the top of the plateau to Flagstaff and far up the slopes of Arizona's tallest landmark, the San Francisco Peaks. Anyone who has worked in a gas station in Flagstaff has had this experience: A certain number of rumpled travelers start in Los Angeles or Albuquerque the evening before and drive through the night on U. S. Route 66, or more recently Interstate 40. At dawn they find themselves in Flagstaff gazing at Mars Hill, Mount Elden, and the sharp outline of the Peaks, which may have a cap of snow. "I thought Arizona was desert," they say.

By daylight there is no surprise. The Peaks are visible for many miles, like cutouts pasted against a usually blue sky. The peaks are sacred to Navajos and Hopis, and a comforting affirmation of faith for the rest of us.

John Hance, a Grand Canyon guide who concocted a body of tall tales, claimed he piled up the Peaks with the dirt left from the digging of the Canyon. But the four San Francisco Peaks are plainly volcanic, as are many of the region's smaller mountains. Geologists say the Peaks were formed by two volcanoes, one a very long time ago, and one comparatively recently, maybe 430,000 years ago. That volcano built a peak 15,000 feet tall. It was a lengthy process of collapse and settling that created the four peaks which now surround an inner basin. The tallest, Humphreys Peak, has settled to a mere 12,670 feet.

Some of Arizona's best-known mountains rise abruptly from the desert, like islands from the sea. Since "desert island" has an entirely different meaning, authors and scientists have come up with a different label for these landmark ranges: "sky islands."

Of these islands in the sky, the Chiricahuas (cheer-uh-COW-was), in the southeast corner of the state, are the best known. Cochise was chief of a tribe known as Chiricahua Apache who lived in these mountains and the nearby Dragoons. In 1871, the U.S. government, seeking peace with Cochise, gave the Apaches a reservation fifty-five miles square, including the Chiricahua and Dragoon mountains and the Sulphur Springs Valley between them.

Cochise died in 1874. Legend says his warriors buried him in or near Cochise Stronghold, the canyon in the Dragoons where Cochise made his headquarters. Following the chief's directions, they rode their horses back and forth over his grave to erase all sign of it.

After the death of Cochise, the Apaches fragmented, and the mountains became a base for raids against Americans and Mexicans. A couple of years after the death of Cochise, the government took back the reservation.

Early editors of *Arizona Highways* frequently printed photographs of Cochise Head, a rock formation in the Chiricahuas that appears to be the profile of an Indian.

The magazine also ran photos of the Wonderland of Rocks, a particularly colorful part of Chiricahua National Monument. The Chiricahuas were formed by successive periods of volcanic action; wind and water have since carved some of the rocks into bizarre shapes. A trail system within the monument allows the visitor to explore these shapes, and perhaps to see a white-tailed deer or a coatimundi.

Other canyons in the Chiricahuas, notably Cave Creek, offer bird-watching of a high order. The Chiricahuas are home to—among other species—the rare, elegant (coppery-tailed) trogon.

Krutch was fascinated by these sky islands and by their suddenness, which was largely a result of their being created in a dry climate. "Around the bases of the mountains is piled the coarser debris in which they are slowly burying themselves," he wrote. "...only where precipitation is low do even the larger fragments from a decaying mountain remain so close to the slopes down which they tumbled.

"From a distance their flanks look almost bare, but near the more humid summits they are often crowned with pines.

"These mountains do much more than please the eye. Every thousand feet means a perceptible change in temperature and rainfall so that the mountains are responsible for the fact, so surprising to the newcomer, that Arizona is astonishingly rich in the number of different plants, animals, and birds native there...one need travel only tens rather than hundreds of miles in the journey from the Sonoran Desert around Tucson to the pine and fir forests which correspond to those found near sea level in southern Canada. To travel a thousand feet upward is, so far as climate is concerned, the approx-

imate equivalent of traveling six hundred miles northward."

The cities of Phoenix and Tucson are rivals, and Tucson usually is given "points" in the fanciful competition for its proximity to the mountains. Still, Phoenix has a series of mountain preserves like no other municipal park system in the world. And while in height the mountains of Phoenix make a chain such as the Laurentians in Canada look like gentle swells on the earth, they are still "desert" mountains with "desert" vegetation.

But from downtown Tucson, it is perhaps a forty-five minute drive northeast to alpine conditions on 9157-foot Mount Lemmon, tallest of the Santa Catalina Mountains. South of Tucson, the Santa Ritas make a similar ascent. There are other islands in the sky: the Huachucas southeast of Tucson, and farther to the northeast, Mount Graham, rising 10,717 feet over the Gila Valley.

Astronomers have put several of the peaks in southern Arizona to modern use. The Smithsonian Institution has located its astrophysical observatory on 8500-foot Mount Hopkins in the Santa Ritas. West of Tucson, the National Optical Astronomy Observatories operate Kitt Peak National Observatory on a 6875-foot mountaintop at the north end of the Baboquivari range.

A similar sky island, Hualapai Peak, rises 8417 feet in northwestern Arizona, just south of Interstate 40. It seems

Astronomy has thrived in Arizona since ancient times. Prehistoric man found amazingly precise ways to measure the solar cycle, which was necessary for ceremonies, planting, and harvesting.

(Above left) Petroglyphs in Painted Rock State Park, believed to be Hohokam, mark the winter solstice, one-eighth year, equinox, and summer solstice by movement of sunlight through an opening in the rocks. Arrival of the shortest day of the year, followed by the longer days, was reassuring to people who lived with the solar system as their only clock. Art Clark

(Above) Percival Lowell, who founded Lowell Observatory at Flagstaff in 1894, is pictured observing the planet Venus on a 24-inch refracting telescope that is still in use. The observatory's astronomers found, in 1913, the first evidence for the modern theory of an expanding universe, and in 1930 the planet Pluto was discovered from Lowell.
Lowell Observatory

(Above right) A cluster of observatories sit atop the Baboquivari Mountains, center of the Papago universe. Scientists working there recently found evidence of another planetary system such as our own. This and other new findings have made scientists question long-held theories on galaxies. National Optical Astronomy Observatories

out of place, but it is within the same basin-and-range geological zone as the peaks of southern Arizona; the Mogollon escarpment, which separates basin and range from plateau formations, curves north and east of Hualapai.

Arizona counts also a number of mountains which fit into no superlative category, yet are distinctive for one peculiarity or another:

The Mazatzal Mountains northeast of Phoenix have never been called anything other than "Mat-a-ZALS." Mazatzal, an Apache word for "bleak, barren," is too much of a mouthful. But they are neither bleak nor barren. With several peaks reaching over 7000 feet, the Mazatzal's lofty slopes are pine covered. And the most southern point of the range, Four Peaks, has yielded some of the most beautiful amethyst imaginable.

The Bradshaw Mountains between Phoenix and Prescott contain remnants of many of the state's more colorful mining ghost towns. It was here a good part of Arizona's raucous history transpired.

Mingus Mountain, just beyond the Bradshaws, still harbors the mining town of Jerome, a semi-ghost that clings precariously to the east face of Cleopatra Hill. From Jerome, and the switchbacks of U. S. Route 89-A above Jerome, the view of the Verde Valley takes away the breath. When the narrow gauge United Verde and Pacific Railway topped Mingus in 1895 to connect the

Jerome copper mines with the outside world, the wheels of its cars carried white dots. Not to measure mileage, as in the case of Crook's military wagon, but so the engineer could look back and see if the wheel was turning, or whether constant braking had locked it up in a "hot box."

East of Phoenix, the face of the Superstitions rises abruptly. Perhaps it was the Indians' dread of the place that resulted in the intriguing name. This is the alleged site of the Lost Dutchman gold mine, the gold of the Peralta family that prospector Jacob Walz supposedly found, then lost again. The search for gold has brought a strange procession of people to the mountains, but the real treasure in the Superstitions seems to be its wilderness area that only hikers and horseback riders may penetrate.

In Yuma County there is a respectable range of mountains known as the Kofas, an acronym for the King of Arizona mine. Palm Canyon, a narrow defile on the west side of the range, contains the only fan palms native to Arizona.

Longtime *Arizona Highways* editor Raymond Carlson wrote: "There is persuasion in the invitation of the cool, green silence of the mountains while summer's heat still envelops the lowlands. In just a couple of whiles from the desert, one can find streams, lakes, meadows, and the eternal music of the pines telling their age-old secrets to the wind."

He could have been describing the White Mountains,

the woods around Flagstaff, or the top of Mingus. His last phrase quickly draws me back forty years or more. For most of this century, a long, unpaved stretch of General Crook's Road has been called the Rim Road. We used to reach it by climbing out of the Verde Valley past Thirteen-mile Rock and Twenty-seven-mile Lake, mileposts that Crook knew.

Just east of Baker Butte, the road skirted the lip of the Rim, letting us see what seemed like half of Arizona spread out below, almost unchanged from when Martha Summerhayes had marveled at it. Just before the road reached Fred Haught Ridge, where a soldier had once carved "V-44" on the blazed face of a ponderosa pine, we turned off to General Springs cabin. General Crook had found this place and liked to camp there. We would stay there for a season, while Dad pursued the wily forest fire.

As he shut down the rhythmic old Chevy engine, the silence was startling. Then we heard the sighing of the pines. It was lonesome background music, so soft yet so pervasive that soon we would notice it only when a shift of the wind, or a sudden calm, changed its delicate pitch.

(Right) Arizona's ghost town landmarks have been a treasure trove to the collectors of old glass. The beauty of their colors, changed by years in the sun, caught the artistic eye of the photographer. David Muench

(Below) Cleopatra Hill formed the backdrop for this 1955 photo taken from the Jerome cemetery. Art Clark

(Bottom) A boarded-up building on Cleopatra Hill in Jerome waits in vain for the mines to reopen. Note San Francisco Peaks in the distance. David Muench

(Preceding panel, pages 64-65) The Superstition Mountains
suggest mystery, partly because of the legend of the Lost
Dutchman mine. Jacob Walz is said to have come into possession
of a map to a Spanish gold mine in the Superstitions,
and to have mined it quietly without ever revealing its location.
The quest for the Lost Dutchman has lured adventurers ever
since, and some have lost their lives there. Much of the range is a
federal wilderness area, not considered inhospitable at all by
seasoned backpackers. This panorama of a winter morning in the
Superstitions was taken from Weaver's Needle, which figures
prominently in the maps which purport to lead to the
Dutchman's gold. Lon McAdam

(Above) An aerial view does little to flatten the rugged
Superstitions; Weaver's Needle is upper center. Jerry Jacka

(Right) Crisp morning air gives clarity to this photo of Miner's
Needle in the Superstition Wilderness Area. Steve Bruno

(Following panel, pages 68-69) Frederic Remington's A Dash
for the Timber, painted in 1889. The best known of
Remington's works, this commissioned painting was based on
notes from an 1886 tour of Arizona in search of Geronimo, and
a journey in 1888 with the 10th Cavalry through the Apache
country of eastern Arizona. Courtesy Amon Carter Museum

A coppery sunset in the White Mountains filters through a picket-like row of ponderosa pines. Hundreds of miles of Arizona's eastern and central mountains are covered with these trees. David Muench

(Inset) A great horned owl glowers at an intruder.
Paul Berquist

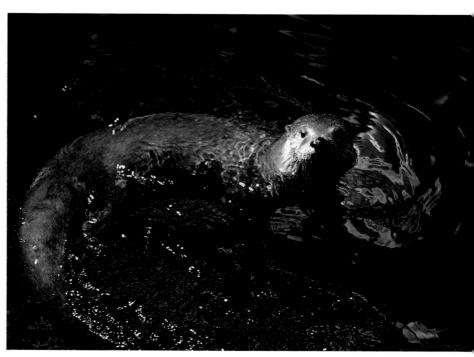

(Left) It's a summer morning on the West Fork of the Little Colorado River, a fisherman's dream stream in the White Mountains. Jerry Sieve

(Below) A river otter enjoys an early morning swim. James Tallon

(Bottom) The homely horned toad dwells in both the mountains and the deserts of Arizona. Jerry Jacka

San Francisco Peaks have a timeless, seemingly magical attraction to many Americans. But to some Arizonans they have spiritual meaning. The Peaks are the home of the Hopi Kachinas (gods) and a point on the Navajo compass. This view, captured in winter by Trevor Stanley, appeared in Arizona Highways in January, 1973.

The McMath Solar Telescope on Kitt Peak is silhouetted against a violent summer storm over the Baboquivari range.

(Inset) Kitt Peak rises 6875 feet out of the Baboquivaris, an island of mountains in the Sonoran Desert. Gary Ladd photos

While Arizona's crystal clear skies attract astronomers, they also invite some photographers to try their luck at photographing at night. Above, star tracks scribe arcs around the center point of the North Star, depicting the symmetry of nature. On a moonless night with no clouds, no airplanes, the right camera equipment, some luck, and lots of patience for the hours-long exposures, interesting results can be achieved. Different colored arcs are caused by different temperatures of the various stars. Close to the horizon, the colors are affected by the density of the atmosphere. Richard Fisher

(Left) Winter's chill grips the 7645-foot-high landmark known as Four Peaks, the southern end of the Mazatzal Range, while the desert basks in sunshine. James Tallon

At the extreme southeastern corner of
Arizona, yucca stalks spike a pastel
evening sky on the east side of the
Chiricahua Mountains.
David Muench

(Inset) A rare bird indeed is the
elegant (coppery tailed) trogon,
member of an elite family of birds
found in the Chiricahuas but few
other areas in the United States.
G. C. Kelley

(Below) Punch and Judy seem to be carrying on their timeless bickering in the cover photo of the July, 1946, Arizona Highways. Punch and Judy are among hundreds of stone caricatures (including Donald Duck) identified in the Wonderland of Rocks, Chiricahua National Monument. But the figures antedate Disney, and probably even the human race, by a vast span of years. That issue of Arizona Highways is a study in the evolution of the magazine, having some vestiges of its early design and comparatively crude reproduction, but offering promise of the quality to come. The July, 1946, issue was devoted to those areas of Arizona then under jurisdiction of the National Park Service, a summer guide to many of the state's better-known landmarks.

(Right) A current photo shows that a mere forty years of erosion have had little effect on Punch and Judy. Willard Clay

(Left) Six decades after Arizona Highways *first printed photographs of the stone profile in repose, Cochise Head watches over the fantastic stone shapes of the Chiricahuas and still challenges photographers who don't normally shoot portraits.*

(Below) A fiery maple in autumn stands apart from the more subdued trees and volcanic rocks of a canyon in the Chiricahuas.

(Following panel, pages 86-87) The volcanic formations of the Kofa Mountains rise out of the desert floor near Yuma in western Arizona. The Kofas took their name from the King of Arizona Mine. The range is a refuge for desert bighorn sheep and a rare variety of palm tree native to the immediate area.
David Muench photos

If Arizonans find serenity on the desert and contentment in the mountains, they get their magic from the canyons of the state. Grand Canyon is the largest (by several powers) and most spectacular of a varied lot.

Every so often, local pride causes someone living in Oak Creek Canyon, or near Salt River Canyon, to claim that the lesser gorge rivals the Grand Canyon. It is a harmless kind of boasting. Some of the other canyons *are* easier to get to know.

Conservationist John Muir, pleading inadequacy, described Grand Canyon thus: "In a hot, dry, monotonous, forested plateau, seemingly boundless, you come suddenly and without warning upon the abrupt edge of a gigantic sunken landscape of the wildest, most multitudinous features, and those features, sharp and angular, are made out of flat beds of limestone and sandstone forming a spiry, jagged, gloriously colored mountain range countersunk in a level gray plain. It is a hard job to sketch it even in scrawniest outline; and try as I may, not in the least sparing myself, I cannot tell the hundredth part of the wonders of its features—the side canyons, gorges, alcoves, cloisters, and amphitheaters of vast sweep and depth, carved in its magnificent walls; the throng of great architectural rocks it contains resembling castles, cathedrals, temples, and palaces, towered and spired and painted, some of them nearly a mile high, yet beneath one's feet. All this, however, is less difficult than to give any idea of the impression of wild, primeval beauty and power one receives in merely gazing from its brink .... It is impossible to conceive what the canyon is, or what impression it makes, from description or pictures, however good .... The prudent keep silence."

Many prudent people have not kept silence. Each proclaims the Canyon indescribable, then tries to describe it. Major John Wesley Powell, who first explored the Colorado River through the Canyon in 1869, kept a diary powerful in its description.

"The gorge is black and narrow below, red and gray and flaring above, with crags and angular projections on the walls, which, cut in many places by side canyons, seem to be a vast wilderness of rocks. Down in these grand, gloomy depths we glide, ever listening, for the mad waters keep up their roar; ever watching, ever peering ahead, for the narrow canyon is winding, and the river is closed in so that we can see but a few hundred yards, and what there may be below we know not; but we listen for falls, and watch for rocks, or stop now and then, in the bay of a recess, to admire the gigantic scenery. And ever, as we go, there is some new pinnacle or tower, some crag or peak, some distant view of the upper plateau, some strange shaped rock, or some deep, narrow side canyon. Then we come to another broken fall, which appears more difficult than the one we ran this morning ...."

Late one night, about a hundred years after Powell's first expedition, a group of us were sitting on a sandy beach in the bottom of the Canyon. We had arrived by rubber raft.

The campfire had died, and the moon was not visible. Yet reflected light from the sandstone cliffs cast an enchanted glow. It was then I felt compelled to explain what I had read somewhere about the reflective properties of sandstone. In the embarrassing silence that followed, I realized that the last thing a spectator wants to know is how magic works.

Nevertheless, naturalist Joseph Wood Krutch explained the why of Grand Canyon without spoiling its magic:

"Why is Grand Canyon unique, or why are such canyons, even on a smaller scale, rare ...? First there must be a thick series of rock strata slowly rising as a considerable river flows over it. Second, that considerable river must carry an unusual amount of hard sand or stone fragments in suspension so that it will be able to cut downward at least as rapidly as the rock over which it flows is rising. Third, that considerable river must be flowing through very arid country. Otherwise, rain, washing over the edges of the cut, will widen it at the top as the cut goes deeper. That is why broad valleys are characteristic of regions with normal rainfall; canyons, large and small, of arid country.

"And Grand Canyon is the grandest of all canyons because at that particular place all the necessary conditions were fulfilled more exuberantly than at any other place in the whole world. The Colorado River carries water from a relatively wet country through a dry

(Far left) Major John Wesley Powell
led the first expedition through the Grand
Canyon in 1869 and explored its length again
in 1871-72. Powell was also a precise but
colorful writer, recounting all his explorations
in diaries and books. Here he is shown with
Tau-Gu, chief of the Paiute Indians. Arizona
Historical Society

(Left) Powell commanded the first exploration
of the Colorado River from this chair on the boat
Emma Dean, named for the major's wife.
Arizona Historical Society

one, it bears with it a fantastic amount of abrasive material, the rock over which it flows has been slowly rising during several millions of years, and too little rain falls to widen very rapidly the gash which it cuts."

In *Grand Canyon*, published in 1957, Krutch wrote, "This is, after all, one of the most visited spots on the face of the Earth. As the Swiss hotel is said to have boasted, 'Thousands come here from all parts of the world seeking solitude.' But at Grand Canyon at least they can find it."

Krutch recommended a slow process of getting acquainted with the Canyon. "The Canyon requires what we call in the lingo of our day 'a double take.' Only that way does its size, its antiquity, or the grandioseness of the forces which made it become real .... First there is the impression of some sort of man-made diorama trying to fool the eye. Only later comes the gradual acceptance of the unbelievable fact."

In 1908, President Theodore Roosevelt declared Grand Canyon a national monument under the Antiquities Act of 1906. Five years earlier, before he had the tools to preserve the Canyon, Roosevelt visited it and issued a plea.

"Leave it as it is. You cannot improve on it; not a bit. The ages have been at work on it, and man can only mar it. What you can do is to keep it for your children, your children's children, and all who come after you, as one of the sights which every American, if he can travel at all, should see."

In the southwest corner of Grand Canyon, Havasu Creek also cut a canyon. The creek exists for only about ten miles from its origin to the point where it joins the Colorado. Yet it has created a red rock canyon frequently described as Arizona's Shangri-la, for lack of more appropriate ways to describe it.

Their gods gave the Havasupai Indians, who number about 400, an Eden in which they built the village of Supai. Downstream, a series of waterfalls carries the blue-green waters of Havasu Creek toward Grand Canyon. The most spectacular of the falls are Navajo, about seventy-five feet tall; Havasu, about 100 feet; and Mooney Falls, a dramatic 196 feet. The water carries travertine, which forms natural dams, hence broad pools, beneath the falls.

Knowing travelers have visited Havasu Canyon since Father Francisco Garcés explored it in 1776. But the quantity and perhaps the quality of visitors have been filtered by the harsh geography. It is a sixty-mile drive from old U.S. Route 66 to Hualapai Hilltop. From there the visitor must cover eight miles by foot or horseback to reach Supai. The first mile and a half of the trail into the canyon is a dizzying series of switchbacks, but few who have made the trip have said it wasn't worth it.

Some localities excuse well-deserved anonymity by calling themselves best-kept secrets. Arizona's best-kept secret is "discovered" regularly. There is nothing furtive about Canyon de Chelly National Monument in northeastern Arizona; millions have visited it. But given its attractions, it's a wonder more have not come.

Canyon de Chelly and its equally colorful tributary, Canyon del Muerto, drain the Chuska Mountains on the Navajo Indian Reservation. The Navajo, who have occupied the canyon for several centuries, still farm the canyon bottom and graze their livestock there in the summer. Today, Navajo guides lead commercial four-wheel-drive tours through the canyons. Some of the guides, driving trucks with fat tires along the sandy canyon bottom, refer to the trip as "shake-and-bake." Sunburned visitors, however, complain mostly of tired eyes when they come back from their trip through the canyons and the ruins.

Cliff dwellings of the early Anasazi peoples have been preserved in the caves and under the overhanging cliffs. Those who don't have time to tour the canyons can drive to overlooks to view several of the ruins, including White House, the best-known Kayenta Anasazi cliff dwelling.

From the time of the Anasazi forward, the occupants of Canyon de Chelly have painted pictographs on the canyon walls. Some of these depict Spanish soldiers; more recent Navajo artists, painting 150 to 200 years ago, left striking figures of animals at Antelope House Ruin and a blue and white cow at Standing Cow Ruin.

Although these may be the most enduring of the artists who have tried to capture Arizona, their work must compete with startling colors applied by Nature. Minerals washed from above have stained the sandstone cliff faces with striped abstracts.

In 1864, when the U.S. Army was trying to subjugate the tribe, Colonel Kit Carson commanded a devastating mission that cleared many Navajos from the canyons. The campaign was a forerunner to the "Long Walk," leading the Navajo into a four-year exile at Fort Sumner, New Mexico.

Where Canyon de Chelly is joined by Monument Canyon, Spider Rock rises 849 feet, half again as tall as the Washington Monument. It is said the mythical Spider Woman lives atop this spire. Navajo children who misbehave are warned she will carry them to her rock and eat them.

In the early years of *Arizona Highways*, the magazine carried frequent progress reports on construction of a road through Oak Creek Canyon, south of Flagstaff. This required the building of switchbacks at the head of the canyon to climb 1500 feet onto the Colorado Plateau. The road, which is now U.S. Route 89-A, was for forty years a main north-south highway in Arizona.

The Mogollon escarpment, which forms the south edge of the plateau, was cracked by faulting ten or twelve million years ago. Oak Creek seized that opportunity to carve a gorge of banded rainbow sandstone and line its bottom with greenery.

Zane Grey, who lived for a time in Oak Creek Canyon, made it well-known by his 1920 novel *Call of the Canyon*. The story dealt with the therapeutic effects of the canyon on a rich New York girl, Carley Burch, and her suitor, a mentally and physically scarred veteran of World War I.

The effects of Oak Creek on Carley are, many years later, entirely believable: "The morning resembled one of the rare Eastern days in June, when the air appeared flooded by rich thick amber light. Only the sun

here was hotter and the shade cooler.

"Carley took to the trail below where West Fork emptied its golden-green waters into Oak Creek. The red walls seemed to dream and wait under the blaze of the sun; the heat lay like a blanket over the still foliage; the birds were quiet; only the murmuring stream broke the silence of the canyon. Never had Carley felt more the isolation and solitude of Oak Creek Canyon. Far indeed from the madding crowd! Only Carley's stubbornness kept her from acknowledging the sense of peace that enveloped her—that and the consciousness of her own discontent. What would it be like to come to this canyon—to give up to its enchantments?"

Not to give away the ending (in case you haven't read the book yet), but Carley found the answers and, apparently, lived happily ever after.

It is to be hoped she invested in real estate. At its mouth, Oak Creek Canyon enters the Verde Valley, which at this point is rimmed with towering red cliffs and studded with buttes of red and gold sandstone. At one time, the red rocks rivaled Monument Valley as a location for Western movies. The community of Sedona infiltrated the red rocks, attracting people who can afford to live where they wish, as well as a sizable art colony. Prominent members of the Cowboy Artists of America have replaced moviemakers as depicters of the Red Rock Country.

The U.S. Forest Service, which has jurisdiction over Oak Creek, may wish the road project of the 1920s had not been quite so successful. The pressure of visitors has threatened to destroy the attractions of Oak Creek Canyon, which is only a dozen miles long. The Forest Service now controls where motorists can leave the highway. (The same kind of pressure has caused restrictions in Sabino

(Above) *This pictograph mural at Standing Cow Ruin in Canyon del Muerto depicts the arrival of Spanish soldiers and missionaries in Navajo country.* Jerry Jacka

(Inset) *White House is the best-known ruin in Canyon de Chelly.* Dick Dietrich

Canyon, a pretty and popular gorge in the Santa Catalina Mountains. For better or for worse, the mouth of Sabino literally opens into a residential area of Tucson.)

Seekers of solitude can still escape the crowds by hiking the West Fork of Oak Creek. Farther west, Sycamore Canyon offers the backpacker or horseback rider nearly 56,000 acres of federally protected wilderness area, much of it vertical. Sycamore has long been one of those best-kept landmark secrets. The federal wilderness designation saved it from mining or other exploitation, but it is so remote human traffic has not been a severe problem. A wilderness hiker may bask in the illusion that he is a discoverer, a pioneer. But Sycamore, and other canyons, frequently offered sheltered homesites for prehistoric people. They built their cliff dwellings high in the canyon walls where hikers may visit them (but not disturb them, for that is a violation not only of good sense, but of federal laws).

Arizona canyons are home to the peregrine falcon. Artist Larry Toschik is well-known for depicting Arizona's colorful birds and is a frequent contributor to Arizona Highways.

Many Arizona canyons have international reputations among bird-watchers (in contrast to fishing canyons, whose fame tends to be only local). Birding is especially good in the southern part of the state. Just south of Tucson, in the Santa Rita Mountains, Madera Canyon has supported birders, researchers in the life sciences, and, until recently, summer home owners.

Some of the other hot spots for birders are Ramsey Canyon in the Huachucas, and Rucker, Turkey Creek, and Cave Creek canyons in the Chiricahuas.

There are at least eight Turkey Creeks in Arizona, named for wild turkeys which used to be more numerous than they are now. Ninety miles northwest of the one in the Chiricahuas, another Turkey Creek is tributary to one of Arizona's most enticing canyons, Aravaipa.

Mention Aravaipa to a backpacker, a conservationist, an old-time Arizonan, or a history buff, and each gets the same kind of knowing gleam in his eye. Aravaipa Creek cut a twelve-mile-long canyon clear through the Galiuro mountain range as the mountains were forming. The craggy sides of the gorge rise 700 to 1200 feet above the creek bed.

In 1969, 4044 acres of the canyon were set aside as a Bureau of Land Management primitive area to protect seven miles of Aravaipa Creek and keep it wild. Then in 1984 it was designated a wilderness area and expanded in size to 6670 acres. The bureau says approximately 200 species of birds have been observed there, including the bald eagle and peregrine falcon. Desert bighorn sheep have been introduced to the area, and hikers occasionally report seeing the shy animals, although that is far less likely than seeing mule deer, coyotes, or the raccoon-like coatimundi.

Aravaipa's other inhabitants include mountain lions, bats that hang out in the canyon's many caves, and—the bureau warns visitors—several species of rattlesnake.

Old Camp Grant was a military post near the mouth of Aravaipa Canyon, where the creek joins the San Pedro River. In 1871, several hundred Apaches had attached themselves to the camp, where they could get food in exchange for work. In Tucson, meanwhile, a vigilante group had formed to put an end to continuing Apache raids throughout southern Arizona. On April 23, the vigilantes marched on the post when the soldiers were away. Historians call it the Old Camp Grant Massacre. According to some accounts, more than 100 Indians were killed, most of them women and children.

Skeleton Canyon, in the extreme southeastern corner of Arizona, was the site of some notable events in Southwestern history. It was the custom of outlaws in unpoliced border areas to set up two-way traffic—steal from Mexicans and sell the loot in the United States, then steal American cattle and hard goods to sell south of the border. The process was even refined further, so that horses stolen in southern Arizona could be sold in the White Mountains, and rustled animals from the mountains were driven back to southeastern Arizona. A gang known as "the cowboys," led by Newman H. "Old Man" Clanton, engaged in this traffic and whatever other lucrative activities caught their eye.

In August of 1881, part of the Clanton gang ambushed a party of Mexican smugglers in a canyon of the Peloncillo Mountains of southeastern Arizona, killing the Mexicans and taking about 4000 dollars in silver bullion and other valuables. They left the bodies where they fell, to become skeletons and give the canyon its name.

A few days later, Old Man Clanton and four of his troops were ambushed and killed as they herded stolen cattle through the canyon. The massacre has traditionally been attributed to Mexican outlaws seeking vengeance. But it could have been a prelude to the famous gunfight at the O. K. Corral, which occurred two months later in Tombstone.

The arch rivals of the Clantons were the five Earp brothers and their cohorts, known around Tombstone as the Dodge City gang. Historian Glenn Boyer has spent years researching the Earps. In a 1982 article in *Arizona Highways*, Boyer suggested that the Dodge City gang had the motive and the opportunity to eliminate Old Man Clanton and thin out his gang.

After Cochise died, many Chiricahua Apaches were confined to reservations. But some refused to give up the old ways. They became fugitives and raiders, operating across the Mexican border. For more than a decade this mobile band frustrated United States and Mexican soldiers who tried to capture them. The sons of Cochise had the hereditary bloodlines to become chief, but not the leadership abilities.

The warrior Geronimo became leader. The fact that he was able to elude capture was a considerable embarrassment to the Army, which put a major force into the field. General George Crook, an unorthodox military leader, audaciously met Geronimo in the mountains in 1883 and convinced him to settle his band on the San Carlos Reservation. As Dan L. Thrapp explained in the May, 1976, *Arizona Highways*, Geronimo eventually grew restless, and, in 1885, slipped away from the sprawling reservation. Then, in March of 1886, Crook and Geronimo met in the Canyon de Los Embudos (Canyon of the Tricksters) just below the border in Mexico. Geronimo again agreed to surrender himself and his band, which had dwindled to thirty-eight.

But the Indians got drunk during the three days of negotiations, and the white man who provided the liquor convinced them they would be killed if they surrendered. Geronimo and his followers fled.

Crook was transferred out of the territory for that failure, and General Nelson A. Miles was sent to run Geronimo to earth. Miles did not want such a transfer on his record, so his pursuit of Geronimo was both relentless and cautious.

(Above) Pioneer Arizona territorial photographer C.S. Fly of Tombstone recorded a meeting in 1886 between Geronimo, facing camera at left, and General Crook, at right in pith helmet and gauntlets. Arizona Historical Society

(Right) Painter Francis H. Beaugureau also depicted one of the several negotiating sessions between Geronimo and Crook. Courtesy Valley National Bank Collection

Finally, on September 4, 1886, Miles' field troops escorted Geronimo's band from Mexico to Skeleton Canyon. When Miles was as certain as he could be of success, he met with Geronimo and accepted the surrender of the band.

The Apaches were deceived, on orders from Washington. Geronimo thought he was agreeing that his Chiricahua Apaches would be sent to Florida for two years, but the exile stretched to twenty-seven years. Geronimo never did return; he died at Fort Sill, Oklahoma, in 1909.

Remote Skeleton Canyon became known more for its history than for its scenic beauty. Mystery, history, seductive beauty—there's a canyon for every purpose. Like wrinkles in the face of a very old person, the canyons give Arizona its character. They are creases in time, pockets in which to hide secrets from the sun, and showcases for the best that nature can do.

The pastel bluffs of Cave Creek Canyon in the Chiricahua
are riddled with caves of varying size, but the canyon is better
the birdlife which draws birders from around the world. Dav

(Inset) A coyote yodels his mournful song. James Tallon

(Far Left) Water boxed in stone shoots through Ramsey Canyon in the Huachuca Mountains of southeastern Arizona. Jack Dykinga

(Inset) A black-chinned hummingbird hovers before a rack of cactus bayonets. The hummers are numerous and varied in and near the Huachuca Range.
G.C. Kelley

(Above) A spindly waterfall in Ramsey Canyon.
Jack Dykinga

(Left) A rare lemon lily blooms in Ramsey Canyon.
Jack Dykinga

(Above) Cottonwood trunks, seeking the sunlight, form foot bridges across Sabino Creek. Sabino Canyon comes out of the abrupt Santa Catalina Mountains into the outskirts of Tucson.   Peter Kresan

(Right) Where the canyon widens, Sabino Creek forms languid pools which reflect vertical cottonwoods backlighted by the more accessible sun. Dianne Dietrich Leis

(Left) Desert bighorn sheep have been reintroduced into Aravaipa Canyon and are thriving there. A fortunate visitor to Aravaipa's federal primitive area may see the wary sheep peering down from a rocky prominence. Jack Dykinga

(Above) A natural arch in the primitive area. Long ago, Aravaipa Creek cut this gorge through the Galiuro Mountains west of Safford in southeastern Arizona. Kathleen Norris Cook

(Above) A ring-tailed cat ventures from the safety of a tree. G.C. Kelley

(Left) The Santa Rita Mountains south of Tucson harbor a number of shaded canyons, habitat for the birds and animals of the region. The best-known is Madera Canyon, also a refuge for the human inhabitants of Tucson and a research station for scientists and naturalists.
Dick Dietrich

(Above) Oh, that Sycamore Canyon. Eight of Arizona's fifteen counties have Sycamore Canyons. The canyon pictured above, the granddaddy of all the Sycamores, is located in both Coconino and Yavapai counties. Much of it is protected by a federal wilderness area and is frequented by seasoned hikers and horseback adventurers. Dick Dietrich

(Right) A gnarled sycamore has been undercut by the stream through another Sycamore Canyon along the Mexican border in Santa Cruz County, near the community of Arivaca. Peter Kresan

(Below) A coatimundi, resembling a raccoon, on the prowl. G.C. Kelley

(Far left) Although it is not one of Arizona's more advertised scenic attractions, Salt River Canyon is a bonus for the traveler who drives U.S. Route 60 through the state. Alan Benoit

(Above) Five road miles down from either rim, this bridge spans the Salt River, a life-giving water supply for more populated parts of the state. Alan Benoit

(Left) Salt River Canyon as it appeared on the cover of the May, 1956, Arizona Highways.

(Following panel, pages 112-113) Aerial view of Oak Creek Canyon, the setting for Zane Grey's The Call of the Canyon and several Western movies. Oak Creek took advantage of faulting along the Mogollon escarpment to carve a gorge through the red and gold layers of sandstone underlying the Colorado Plateau. Dick Canby

**ARIZONA
HIGHWAYS**
MAY 1959
FORTY CENTS
IN THIS ISSUE:
Sedona-Oak Creek Country

Fans of late-night Westerns on television may recall more than one cavalry troop, or stagecoach, splashing across Red Rock Crossing on Oak Creek near Sedona. Cathedral Rocks form the backdrop.
Bob Clemenz

(Inset) The familiar scene as it appeared on the May, 1959, cover of Arizona Highways.

(Preceding panel, pages 116-117) The turning leaves of vines and ferns rise above polished stones on the floor of Oak Creek Canyon. Nature lovers and photographers in Arizona's desert cities pass the word when the leaves turn in Oak Creek and at higher elevations—an annual spectacle. Larry Ulrich

(Above) A summer thundershower darkens the sky beyond Canyon de Chelly on the Navajo Reservation. James Tallon

(Right) White House Ruin tucked in its niche beneath the varnished cliffs of Canyon de Chelly, from the October, 1965, Arizona Highways cover.

(Far right) The same scene twenty years later. The National Park Service has removed some vegetation to reveal lower ruins at White House, not visible in the 1965 photograph. James Tallon

(Following panel, pages 120-121) Canyon de Chelly in winter. Spider Rock rises 849 feet at the junction of de Chelly and Monument canyons in Canyon de Chelly National Monument. Navajo children are told that if they misbehave, Spider Woman will drag them in her lair atop the spire and eat them, leaving only their bones. Peter Kresan

Mummy Cave in Canyon del Muerto was occupied from about A.D. 300 to 1300. Mummy Cave Overlook is accessible by automobile; the cave itself is near the end of a long jeep tour Jerry Jacka

(Inset) The wall of this Kiva shows remnants of symbolic paintings. David Muench

(Above) Thomas Moran's Chasm of the Colorado, *oil on canvas, is itself a national treasure.* Courtesy National Museum of American Art, Smithsonian Institution

(Left) *A similar view in winter from the Grandview Trail on the Grand Canyon's South Rim.* Kathleen Norris Cook

(Right) *The walls of the Watchtower at Desert View Overlook are little more vertical than those of the Canyon. This notable landmark was designed in 1932 by Mary E. J. Colter. Murals in the tower's second level, by Hopi artist Fred Kabotie, depict the Snake Legend — a story about a Hopi boy who floated through the Canyon in a hollow log hundreds of years before Major John Wesley Powell's expedition in 1869.* Tom Till

(Following panel, pages 126-127) *Remote Toroweap Overlook, from the north side of Grand Canyon. Accessible only by dirt roads of the Arizona Strip, Toroweap is west of the better-known areas of the North Rim.* David Muench

(Above) Dams on the Colorado River have changed the nature of some rapids, but have done little to tame Lava Falls, highest navigable rapids in the world. Ken Easley

(Left) Rising waters of Lake Mead have considerably shortened Emory Falls since this scene appeared on the February, 1938, Arizona Highways cover.

(Far left) From Lees Ferry to Lake Mead, the canyons of the Colorado River contain a succession of rapids, tributary canyons, and waterfalls not seen by visitors to the two accessible rims. But for more than a century explorers have been visiting and charting the canyon wonders. Alan Benoit

ARIZONA HIGHWAYS
FEBRUARY · · · · · 1938

Arizona's Shangri-la, Havasu Canyon, is known for spectacular falls which feed pools terraced by travertine deposits. Havasu Falls is one of the prettier cascades. David Muench

(Top right) Pools near the mouth of Havasu Creek are a popular stopping place for Colorado River runners. Wesley Holden

(Center right) Another side canyon to the Colorado, Matkatamiba, provides a pleasant hike and many unique "discoveries." Wesley Holden

(Bottom right) A "warm shower" at Stone Creek Canyon brings welcome relief from the chilly fifty-degree waters of the Colorado. Jerry Jacka

There probably are scientists in the Southwest who would trade their university tenure for a trip back in time to A.D. 1300 or 1400. About that time several different cultures were interrupted, leaving their dwellings and rubbish piles to beguile archaeologists. Anthropologists suspect that remnants of some collapsing cultures, including the Sinagua, joined the Hopis.

The plateau is a complicated place and, as far as man is concerned, its greatest complication has been the Colorado River. For several hundred miles, the Colorado runs through an unbroken series of canyons. At its east end Grand Canyon joins Marble Canyon, Marble adjoins Glen Canyon, Glen leads into Cataract Canyon, and so on. This has been, to say the least, a barrier to north-south travel.

In 1776, Father Silvestre Vélez de Escalante, missionary at Zuñi, and Father Francisco Atanasio Dominguez traveled north and west, seeking a route to the California missions. They became discouraged in the vicinity of Great Salt Lake and turned back south. After trying to cross the Colorado River in several places, Escalante and Dominguez established a steep crossing that is now under the waters of Lake Powell. It was known as Crossing of the Fathers, or Ute Crossing.

The next significant movement of people across the river came in the 1860s and 70s as members of the Church of Jesus Christ of Latter-day Saints (Mormons) moved south through Utah and into Arizona. The pathfinder for this movement was Jacob Hamblin, a missionary and explorer, who built strong ties with the Indians in the region. Hamblin founded a number of communities (and families) including Kanab, Utah, and Alpine, Arizona.

Hamblin used Crossing of the Fathers, but it was far east of the Mormon Road that he was establishing. In 1864, he crossed at a more logical place, where the Paria River joined the Colorado. The place became Lees Ferry, and it served for seventy years.

Lees Ferry was named for John Doyle Lee, at one time a leader in the LDS church in southern Utah and a controversial figure in the history of the West. He was accused of being a principal in the Mountain Meadows Massacre in southwestern Utah in 1857. A band of immigrants from the Midwest was slaughtered, possibly by Paiutes, possibly by Mormons dressed as Paiutes, probably by a combination of the two.

Lee, the only man prosecuted for the massacre, was taken back to Mountain Meadows in 1877 and executed by a firing squad. The justice of his conviction is still questioned. During most of the twenty years between massacre and execution, Lee was a fugitive, moving from place to place in northern Arizona and southern Utah.

In December of 1871, Lee moved to the Colorado River crossing at the mouth of Paria Canyon and established an outpost that his seventeenth wife, Emma, named Lonely Dell. Although Lee's status with the LDS church was clouded, he established Lees Ferry in partnership with Hamblin and with the blessings of church president Brigham Young.

Three uncommon men left their tracks on the Colorado Plateau and its strategic crossroad, Lees Ferry.

(Far left) Jacob Hamblin, "the Mormon Pathfinder," explored the region and established the Mormon Road to carry colonizers from the Church of Jesus Christ of Latter-day Saints into northern and eastern Arizona. Arizona Historical Society

(Center) Members of Major John Wesley Powell's second expedition down the Colorado River repair their boats at Gunnison on the Green River at the start of the 1871 adventure. Arizona Historical Society

(Right) John D. Lee, a tragic figure in Western history, established Lees Ferry at a river crossing located by Hamblin. The ferry served for seventy years as the link that held the region together. Arizona Historical Society

Major John Wesley Powell led the first boat party through the Grand Canyon in 1869 and repeated the trip in 1871-72. Members of the second expedition wrote in their diaries of the hospitality and good food at Lonely Dell.

Lee had not yet established the ferry in 1870 when Major Powell, in the company of Jacob Hamblin, visited the place. Powell made an overland trip that year from the mountains of southern Utah to Fort Wingate, New Mexico. Part of his mission was to find supply points for the following year's river expedition, but Powell also was a diligent explorer of the plateau. The party traveled eastward from Pipe Spring, Arizona, over the Kaibab Plateau and along the Vermilion Cliffs which parallel the Colorado on the north side.

Powell wrote, "On the last day of September, we follow the Vermilion Cliffs around to the mouth of the Paria. Here the cliffs present a wall of about 2000 feet in height—above, orange and vermilion, but below, chocolate, purple, and gray in alternating bands of rainbow brightness ....

"At night we camp on the bank of the Colorado River on the same spot where our boat party had camped the year before. Leaving the party in charge of Mr. Graves and Mr. Bishop, while they are building a ferryboat, I take some Indians to explore the canyon of the Paria."

Three days later, Powell wrote, "The boat is finished, and a part of the camp freight has been transported across the river. The next day the remainder is ferried over, and the animals are led across, swimming behind the ferryboat in pairs. Here a bold bluff more than 1200 feet in height has to be climbed, and the day is spent in getting to the summit. We make a dry camp, that is, without water, except that which has been carried in canteens by the Indians."

Lee began his ferry business with that flat-bottomed scow that Powell's men built, the *Cañon Maid*. Because Lee was a fugitive, and perhaps because he was polygamous, he did not stay in one place long. Emma ran the ferry in his absence. When Lee was arrested in 1874, the LDS church sent Warren D. Johnson and his family to help run the ferry. The Johnsons operated the ferry after the church bought Emma Lee's interest.

It was the only place a wagon or automobile could cross the Colorado between Pearce Ferry, 280 miles downstream (now under Lake Mead), and Hite Ferry, Utah, about 200 miles upstream. It was many more miles in each direction to a bridge.

At the time *Arizona Highways* was founded in 1925, Coconino County was operating Lees Ferry as a public convenience. In 1927, the Arizona Highway Department contracted for a steel arch bridge over Marble Canyon five miles below the ferry. *Arizona Highways* reported on the construction of the Lees Ferry Bridge, later named Navajo Bridge, and its dedication in 1929.

An estimated 5000 people, including governors of four states, traveled rough roads to attend the dedication. Arizona Governor John C. Phillips told them, "Today marked the dawn of the new epoch in the history of the Southwest. Man has achieved another triumph over grim Nature...."

A pilot representing Union Oil Company flew a light plane under the bridge. The dedication party lasted two days; most of the celebrants camped out.

Through the early 1930s, *Arizona Highways* carried frequent accounts of the building of U.S. Route 89 across the Colorado and into the land called the Arizona Strip.

The Strip is the part of Arizona north of the Colorado River. If state boundaries were logical, the Strip would belong to Utah, which tried to annex it in 1897. Completion of Navajo Bridge and U.S. Route 89 shortened the long, lonesome journey from Flagstaff to Utah. Even today, though, it's a hard trip. It is only about ten miles across Grand Canyon from the village at the South Rim to North Rim Lodge. But by highway, it is something over 200 miles.

The only way to drive to the North Rim is by State Route 67, which leaves U.S. Route 89-A at Jacob Lake (named for Hamblin) and crosses the Kaibab Plateau. The heavily forested Kaibab National Forest is on the Strip, but not of it. Even residents of the Strip consider it a separate entity, a world of its own. Its large herds of mule deer have been famous since the days of Theodore Roosevelt. The tassel-eared Kaibab squirrel, peculiar to the plateau, is a subspecies of the Abert squirrel found south of Grand Canyon.

The rest of the Strip falls away from the Kaibab. It is a land of mostly unpaved roads and unexpected sights. Major Powell liked Pipe Spring, and his friend Jacob

Hamblin is credited with its founding. Hamblin's brother Bill, who liked to be called "Gunlock Bill," gave the spring its name. On a dare, Hamblin shot through the bowl of a friend's pipe and knocked the bottom out. The friend wisely had taken the pipe from his mouth and placed it on a rock prior to the demonstration of marksmanship.

A stone fort was built over the spring in 1870 to protect the water supply, as well as a church-owned cattle herd, and the trail that brought colonizers into Arizona. In 1923, Steven Mather, first director of the National Park Service, persuaded President Warren G. Harding to declare the fort a national monument. Now restored, Pipe Spring is operated as a "living museum," with help from Strip residents, descendants of Mormon pioneers.

Toroweap, a remote and beautiful section of the west end of Grand Canyon, can only be reached by an unpaved road across the Strip. The Toroweap Cliffs have enchanted photographers for several decades. The area is known locally as Tuweep, the name of the National Park Service outpost at the end of a lonely gravel road.

Paria Canyon originates in Utah, crosses the border as a shallow wash, then abruptly cuts deep into the plateau. It is a favorite of hikers and photographers who like a real challenge, but John D. Lee was not so enchanted by Paria. In his diary, he told of driving a herd of cattle through the canyon to Lonely Dell.

"We concluded to drive down the creek, which took us some 8 days of toil, fatuige, and labour, through brush, water, ice, and quicksand and some time passing through narrow chasms with perpendicular Bluffs on both sides, some 3000 feet high, and without seeing the sun for 48 hours...."

Lee told of trying to keep track of a sack of seed corn which was "Baptised as often as I was."

After crossing the Colorado at Lees Ferry, early travelers followed the Echo Cliffs south toward the Little Colorado. Powell wrote in 1870, "All day long we pass by the foot of the Echo Cliffs, which are in fact a continuation of the Vermilion Cliffs. It is still a landscape of rocks, with cliffs, pinnacles and towers and buttes on the left, and deep chasms running down into Marble Canyon on the right."

U.S. Route 89 follows that same track. But the northern portion of the route became U.S. 89-Alternate at the end of the 1950s, when a new U.S. Route 89 was built over the Echo Cliffs to Page and Glen Canyon Dam. The route to Utah by way of the dam is a smoother, faster route. The traveler trades an intimate drive along the foot of the Vermilion Cliffs and over the Kaibab for the view of the dam and Lake Powell. Lees Ferry is now protected by the National Park Service. It serves both as a historic site and a launching point for

The Arizona Strip, for all its remoteness — perhaps because of it — has attracted some of the more imposing personalities in Arizona's past. Writer Sharlot Hall, Arizona's remarkable historian in territorial days, set out by wagon in 1911 to explore the Strip, then still so little understood that she was warned not to go. But in the company of guide Allen Boyle of Flagstaff she toured the land north of the Colorado River for more than two months.

(Above left) This stout team and wagon carried Sharlot Hall and her guide across the Strip. Sharlot Hall Museum

(Above) For the inauguration of Calvin Coolidge, Hall wore a turquoise-colored gown with a shawl and purse woven of copper fibers, one of her ways of constantly promoting Arizona. Sharlot Hall Museum

hundreds of raft trips down the Colorado River.

Not all early explorers loved the region as Powell did. Lieutenant Joseph C. Ives crossed the region in 1853-54 and again in 1858. On the second trip, he also took a steamboat 530 miles up the Colorado from its mouth. In a report published in 1861, he wrote, "Ours has been the first and doubtless will be the last party of whites to visit this profitless locality. It seems intended by nature that the Colorado River, along the greater portion of its lonely and majestic way, shall be forever unvisited and undisturbed."

For all its spectacle, the vast Colorado Plateau comprises mostly high desert, and the supply of plateau seems to exceed the immediate demand. But just when the horizon becomes monotonous, a new splash of color appears. The Painted Desert is a specific location at the north end of Petrified Forest National Park, easily accessible to the tourist routes of the last hundred years. But the name Painted Desert applies to a broader geologic region. The rainbow colored hills, the colored bands of sand and sandstone, hopscotch across the plateau, appearing almost at random.

Captain Sitgreaves wrote of finding petrified wood on September 28, 1851, as he passed the site of the present national park. "The ground was strewed with pebbles of agate, jasper, and chalcedony, and masses of what appeared to have been stumps of trees petrified into jasper, beautifully striped with bright shades of red (the predominating color), blue, white, and yellow."

The logs petrified here were washed down from a highland to the south. The logs, and some stumps upright on the site, were covered over with enough silt and volcanic ash to retard their decay. Instead, their cells were replaced with minerals.

Over time the logs were at first deep underground, then exposed by erosion. White men found they made excellent curiosities, and by 1900 the petrified logs were being broken up and carted off at an alarming rate. Arizona conservationists lobbied for protection. Petrified Forest National Monument was set aside in 1906, and a portion of the Painted Desert was added in 1932. The area became a national park in 1962.

The northeastern corner of Arizona is occupied by two jurisdictions, one inside the other. When the exiled Navajo were allowed, in 1868, to return from Fort Sumner, New Mexico, the first of fourteen contiguous blocks of reservation in Arizona was set aside for their use; other land was set aside in Utah and New Mexico. The reservation grew to be about the size of West Virginia, with the largest portion in Arizona.

The Navajo Tribe, which prefers it be called the Navajo Nation, estimates its reservation population at 200,000. The reservation's demographics are tilted from the relatively uptown capital at Window Rock, on the east end, to a primitive style of living along the Echo Cliffs at the west end.

Navajo population centers are only relatively "urban"; there is plenty of elbow room in places like Window Rock or Chinle, which seem to have no centers. Many people are scattered thinly over much more space than later Americans used in their communities. Sometimes a Navajo town seems more like a concept than a place.

The Navajo frequently are mislabeled nomads. They *are* mobile, because much of their economy has been tied to the grazing of sheep upon the thin, fragile soil of the arid plateau.

A Navajo may be happiest when connected to his land, although it is not "his" in the sense of ownership.

Remote, vast, magnificent. The weathered landmarks of Monument Valley provide a sublime panorama of red-rock sculpture unequalled anywhere. Navajo Tribal Park in northeastern Arizona. Ray Manley Studios

He orients himself by way of sacred sites and revered landmarks. This sense of the land has caused some problems with the Hopi, who feel the same way but use the land differently.

In 1882, President Chester A. Arthur established by executive order a rectangular Hopi reservation, within the land that was rapidly becoming Navajo reservation. A few Navajo already were living in the area, and that resulted in a bitter land dispute that is still being untangled.

Most Hopi communities are pueblos perched on three mesas. Hopi farms and religious sites tend to be off the mesas, in the broad valleys and washes.

While other communities were abandoned in the 1300-1400 period, the Hopi village of Oraibi thrived. It was there when Coronado's lieutenants visited in 1540, when Jacob Hamblin proselytized the Hopi in the 1860s, and when Major Powell hiked through in 1870. Powell wrote, "Oraibi is a town of several hundred inhabitants. It stands on a mesa or little plateau 200 or 300 feet above the surrounding plain.... The streets of the town are quite irregular, and in a general way run from north to south. The homes are constructed to face the east. They are of stone laid in mortar, and are usually three or four stories high...."

The Hopi, who now number about 8000, have gained admiration for their industry, their humor, and their serene demeanor. Perhaps they are best known for their complex spiritual life and the dances which it generates. The snake dance has always captured the imagination, but it is one of many beautiful dances that allow the Hopi to stay in tune with the universe. Tradition says the Hopi and Navajo don't get along very well, but some of the most respectful spectators at a Hopi butterfly dance are the Navajo who drop by.

Only at Four Corners do four of the United States meet. Three of the corners, excepting Colorado's, are on the Navajo reservation.

West of Four Corners, Monument Valley straddles the Arizona-Utah border. As with much of the plateau, there is a feeling of fantasy about the sandstone spires and buttes. One of the artists attracted to the area was John Ford, who came here in 1939 to film *Stagecoach* with John Wayne.

(Right) Monument Valley's incomparable landscape has become known to millions of moviegoers largely through the work of Director John Ford. David Muench

(Below) Talking over a scene on the set of The Searchers, 1955, are, from left, John Wayne, John Ford, Monument Valley trading post owner Harry Goulding, and Ward Bond. Herb and Dorothy McLaughlin

(Bottom) Ward Bond leads a group of cowboys during the filming of The Searchers. Herb and Dorothy McLaughlin

Arizona Highways has visited Monument Valley frequently. The entire April, 1956, issue was devoted to the valley and the Navajo who live there. In the September, 1981, issue, William R. Florence wrote an article titled "John Ford...the Duke and Monument Valley." It told how Ford returned to the valley nine times to make such films as *She Wore A Yellow Ribbon, Fort Apache,* and *The Searchers.*

One of the best works on Monument Valley is a thin book by Richard E. Klinck, *Land of Room Enough and Time Enough,* first published in 1953. People who don't know the Triassic from the Mezzanine have found in Klinck's book a clear picture of the forces that shaped Monument Valley: ancient seas depositing thick layers of rocks, violent earth movements lifting them up, relentless erosion carving them into monuments.

Relatively hard rock caps the sandstone monuments. Thus Nature wears away the sides of the monuments without appreciably reducing their height. And a paragraph from Klinck might serve as a caprock for any description of the Colorado Plateau:

"You can watch Nature unleash one of its powerful tools when a great thunderstorm invades the valley. Dormant washes suddenly become alive as silt-filled waters pour down them. Waterfalls spring from everywhere. And the companion tool, never-dying wind, is there still, too, continuing to take its slow but eternal toll of the monuments. But even though you watch carefully you cannot see the effects. The valley of the monuments looks today almost as it did at the time of Christ. There have been only minor changes. After all, what is two thousand years compared to twenty-five million?"

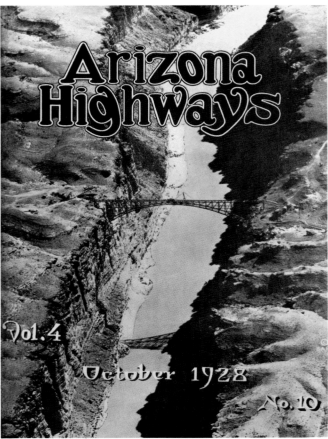

(Above) An aerial view of Navajo Bridge under construction appeared on the October, 1928, Arizona Highways cover. The two halves of the 616-foot steel arch bridge had just been joined, a dizzying 467 feet above the river. The top photograph shows Navajo Bridge as it appears today. The landmark has served travelers to this remote region of Arizona for more than sixty years. Gary Ladd

(Left) The Colorado River at Lees Ferry reflects the bright hues of the Vermilion Cliffs, which have appealed to explorers since Major Powell. David Muench

(Above) Paria Canyon comes into the Arizona Strip from Utah as a sandy wash, rapidly becoming a narrow, deep gorge before joining the Colorado River at Lees Ferry. In his writings, Major Powell used Paria as an example of how a plateau country "box canyon" is formed.
Peter Kresan

(Right) A hiker pauses where a shaft of sunlight penetrates the shadows of a Paria side canyon. Gary Ladd

(Below) The stone fort and post office at Lees Ferry, remnants from the Crossing's turbulent past. Bill Daniels

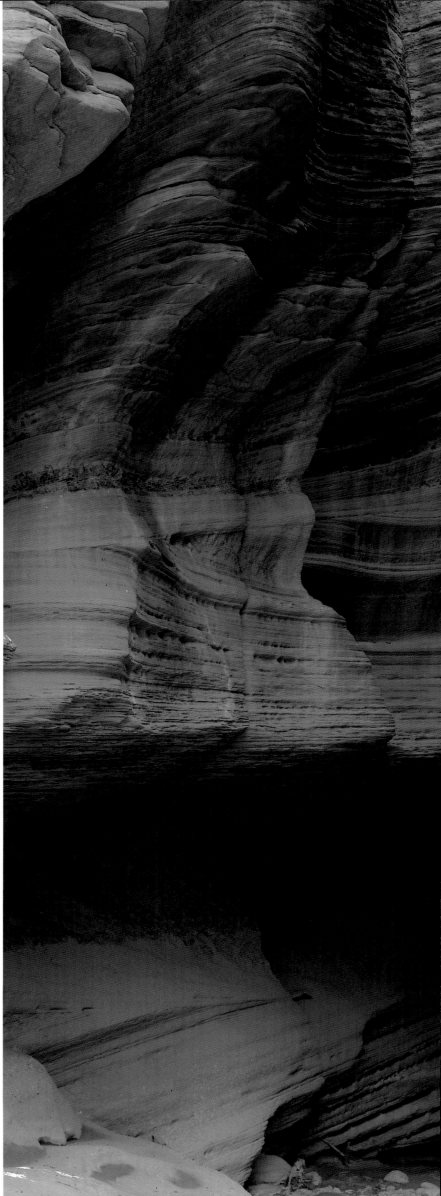

This panorama captures much of the essence of the plateau: a sliver of Lake Powell, sandstone formations rising to Tower Butte, and a storm over distant Navajo Mountain.

(Inset) Looking like stylized petroglyphs, the shadows of mischievous backpackers play on a canyon wall. Gary Ladd photos

(Above) Natural arches in sandstone abound on the Colorado Plateau. This is White Mesa Arch in the remote western portion of the Navajo Reservation; a traditional hogan, seldom seen these days, is in the foreground. David Muench photos

(Right) The circular kiva at Keet Seel was an underground ceremonial chamber of the ancients who lived here. One of the largest and best-preserved Anasazi ruins in Navajo National Monument, Keet Seel apparently attracted a variety of peoples from A.D. 950 to about 1300.

(Above) The landmark known as Window Rock, along Arizona's eastern border, dominates the horizon above the community of the same name. This is also home for the Navajo Tribal Council, which represents America's largest Indian tribe. David Muench

(Right) "Pottery Keeper," by R.C. Gorman. The Heard Museum, the Southwest's premier showcase of primitive art, also displays the work of contemporary artists. Gorman may jet off to San Francisco or Paris; yet he is steeped in the tradition of his people. Although contemporary, his work evokes emotions much as do the ancient petroglyphs of his Canyon de Chelly birthplace. Courtesy the Heard Museum.

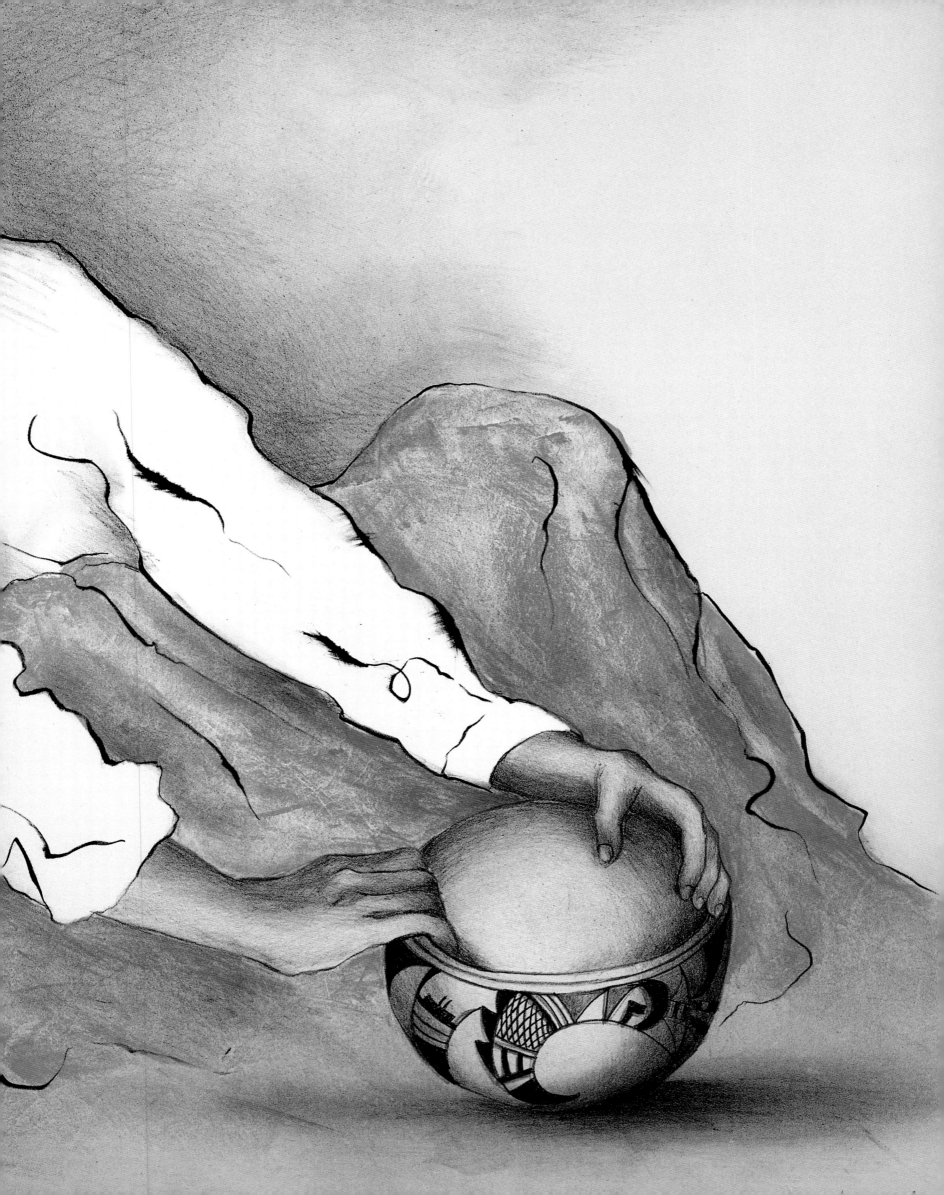

It is difficult for modern-day peoples to understand the depth, complexity, and origins of Hopi culture. The Hopi were firmly established atop their three sacred mesas in northeastern Arizona hundreds of years before the Spanish first arrived in 1540. Hopi stories of ancient migrations, their determination to follow the Hopi Way, the peaceful way, and their rocky villages past and present are like a riddle, wrapped in a mystery, wrapped in an enigma.

(Above) Wearing a traditional dress called a manta, her hair styled in a maiden's whorl — once the symbol of an eligible unmarried Hopi girl — Carol Dawahoya patiently grinds corn in a ceremonial manner.
Jerry Jacka

(Right) Prehistoric ruins of Wupatki National Monument near Flagstaff. Anthropological evidence indicates this was one of the stopping places mentioned in the migration stories of the Hopi. Chuck Place

The Hopi are farming people, and in this high desert land water means life. This painting represents a non-Kachina rain-bringing ceremony called Palhikwtiva, which at the village of Shungopavi, takes place in the spring. It is performed by the Maraw Society, a women's ceremonial organization. The women are wearing elaborate wooden headdresses representing cloud mountains topped with downy eagle feathers. This watercolor, painted the same year Arizona Highways printed its first edition, 1925, is titled Butterfly (water drinking) Dance. The artist, Fred Kabotie, is one of America's best known Native American painters. Courtesy the Heard Museum

Fred Kabotie

(Far left) Pipe Spring National Monument in a 1984 photo by James Tallon, and, at left, as it appeared in the March, 1957, Arizona Highways photo by Willis Peterson. Note that the National Park Service restoration of the historic Mormon fort eliminated the windows seen in the 1957 photo.

(Above) A pole corral on the Arizona Strip near Pipe Spring. Peter Bloomer

(Following panel, page 160) The August, 1940, Arizona Highways center spread was a full-color, four-page fold-out map. It was entitled "A Friendly Guide for the Traveler," and George Avey's illustrations colorfully portrayed the scenic grandeur and numerous points of interest. As an indication of the state's phenomenal growth, the sixth largest city, Scottsdale, wasn't even shown on the 1940 map. Today, Arizona Highways annually publishes more than one million road maps for free distribution to travelers throughout the state.

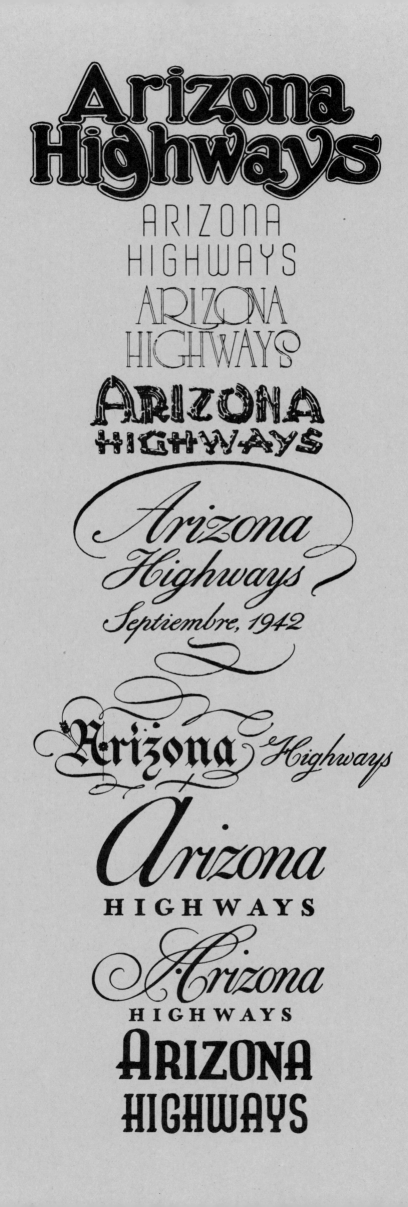

Arizona Highways

ARIZONA HIGHWAYS

ARIZONA HIGHWAYS

ARIZONA HIGHWAYS

Arizona Highways
Septiembre, 1942

Arizona Highways

Arizona
HIGHWAYS

Arizona
HIGHWAYS

ARIZONA
HIGHWAYS